Using Student Feedback to Improve Learning Materials

Using Student Feedback to Improve Learning Materials

MICHAEL B. NATHENSON and
EUAN S. HENDERSON

CROOM HELM   LONDON

© 1980 Michael B. Nathenson and Euan S. Henderson
Croom Helm Ltd, 2-10 St John's Road, London SW11

British Library Cataloguing in Publication Data

Nathenson, Michael B
    Using student feedback to improve learning materials.
    1. Teaching — Aids and devices
    I. Title II. Henderson, Euan S
    371.3'078   LB 1027

ISBN 0-7099-0250-6

Printed in Great Britain by
Biddles Ltd, Guildford, Surrey

CONTENTS

FIGURES

JOURNAL TITLES ABBREVIATED IN BIBLIOGRAPHY

American Journal of Physics
Audio-Visual Communications Review
Audiovisual Instruction
British Journal of Educational Technology
Educational Leadership
Educational Research Bulletin
Educational Screen and Audiovisual Guide
Educational Technology
Harvard Educational Review
Illinois Teacher of Home Economics
Improving Human Performance Quarterly
Journal of Applied Behavioral Analysis
Journal of Curriculum Studies
Journal of Educational Measurement
Journal of Educational Television
Journal of the National Society for Performance and Instruction
Journal of Programed Instruction
Journal of Research and Development in Education
Journal of University Film Producers' Association
Nation's Schools
Programed Instruction
Programmed Learning and Educational Technology
Psychological Reports
Public Telecommunications Review
Review of Educational Review
School Review
Studies in Educational Evaluation
Teachers College Record

To Lynn, Zoë and Eli,
Irini, Chris and Anna

PREFACE

The use of self-instructional learning materials, presented through a wide range of media, is becoming an increasingly pervasive and important part of the educational scene at all levels, from infant school to university. Much has been written, both theoretical and practical, about various aspects of the techniques for developing such materials. However, one phase of the development process, while generally recognised to be critical in producing materials of high quality and educational effectiveness, has been relatively neglected in the literature. This is the phase of trying out the materials in draft form on students, collecting feedback, and undertaking revision in the light of the data so collected. This is sometimes described as *formative evaluation*, and Baker (1974b) has rightly observed that:

> Formative evaluation has reached the status of other laudable endeavors in the field of education – many people talk about it, but few do it right. It is easy to see how formative evaluation came about, for its common sense quality is overwhelming. . .Without a careful integration of formative evaluation activity, instructional development is nothing but an art form, an invention, usually with poor marks in aesthetics.

This book is the product of the authors' experience in planning and executing the collection of feedback from students on self-instructional learning materials concerned with various subject-matters and presented through various media, both printed and audiovisual. It advocates a particular approach to the process of trying out draft materials, which is briefly outlined by means of a case study in Chapter 4. Some readers may find it useful to obtain an overview of the author's approach by beginning their examination of the book with this chapter.

Chapter 1 provides a brief survey of the rise of materials-based learning in order to set the use of student feedback in context, and attempts to sort out some of the terminology in common use. Chapters 2, 3, 5 and 6 take the reader step by step through all the stages of the try-out process, from initial planning of the project to final revision of the materials. The final chapter examines whether using student feedback to revise learning materials can actually improve their educational quality and effectiveness, with special reference to the approach described in Chapters 2-6. The book therefore combines a comprehensive review of what is known about this important phase of developing learning materials (supported by a full bibliography), with a 'how to do it' guide for practitioners which has itself been subjected to extensive try-out.

It is conventional for authors to declare in their prefaces that their work would not have been possible without the aid of many other people. In our case, to say this is no mere bowing to convention. The evaluation of draft learning materials depends upon the full co-operation and commitment of their authors. Equally, such evaluation is impossible without the goodwill and perseverance of the students who try out the materials. We have been privileged to work with a very great number of colleagues, especially academic staff and students of the Open University, without whom, truly, none of the work which led up to the writing of this book would have been possible. Amongst so large a number of active collaborators, it is invidious to mention names. None the less, we take pleasure in recording our great appreciation of the assistance of Frances Berrigan, Mary Geffen, Barbara Hodgson, Ellie Mace, Barbara Mayor-Zand and Derek Rowntree, who have either worked with us on feedback projects, or have made helpful comments and suggestions on individual chapters of this book, or (in the case of Ellie Mace) both. Any shortcomings in the finished product, however, are our responsibility rather than theirs. In particular, we apologise/apologize to the reader for any undetected schizophrenia of style resulting from our joint authorship bridging the two sides of the Atlantic. Finally, the book could not have reached this form without the sterling service rendered by our secretaries, Barbara Kinsella and Marilyn Thompson, whose skill and patience made sense of the many preliminary drafts.

Euan S. Henderson
Michael B. Nathenson
May 1979

1 STUDENT FEEDBACK IN PERSPECTIVE

Any competent teacher, whatever place in the educational system he occupies, makes use of student feedback to improve his effectiveness. Having given a particular lecture or having taught a particular class once, he will incorporate his experiences, consciously or unconsciously, into a 'repeat performance'. Then, providing his interpretation of the feedback from the first occasion is correct, his teaching on the second and subsequent occasions will be more effective. Indeed, even within the context of a single teaching event, the sensitive teacher is continuously receiving and interpreting student feedback, verbal and non-verbal, and modifying his teaching tactics as he goes along. Thus, if students' questions about a particular example of a concept being taught indicate lack of understanding he may inject an additional example, or if blank looks greet part of his exposition he may 'say it again in another way'.

The process of trial and improvement is essential to all teaching. This would presumably not be so if a comprehensive theory of learning existed from which to derive teaching strategies. If there were such a theory, the teacher could deduce from it a plan for each teaching even in advance, knowing that he could achieve maximal effectiveness at the first attempt. But there is not, and it may well be that in the nature of things there never can be a complete theory. Teaching must therefore be an empirical endeavour: using the bits and pieces of partial theories which are available, the teacher constructs the best teaching event he can, tries it out and, in so far as it fails, improves it on the basis of experience. This was recognised by Tyler (1949), who argued that:

As materials and procedures are developed, they are tried out, their inadequacies identified, suggested improvements indicated; there is replanning, redevelopment and then reappraisal; and in this kind of continuing cycle, it is possible for the curriculum and the instructional program to be continuously improved over the years.

Learning Materials and the Teacher's Role

It will be noticed that Tyler referred not only to teaching procedures, but also to teaching *materials*, thus foreshadowing an important change of emphasis in the teacher's role. In the last few decades there has been a considerable shift from an approach to the teacher's role which may be encapsulated in 'telling the students what they need to know' to a role of helping students to learn on their own. Rather than acting as the sole learning resource himself, the teacher has increasingly become the 'manager' of a wide range of alternative learning resources.

The origins of this new role are complex and interwoven, but three elements can be distinguished: (i) concern for the individualisation of learning; (ii) recognition of the importance of 'learning how to learn'; and (iii) technological developments.

The concern for individualisation can be traced back at least to the early years of this century, when some disillusionment was already being expressed with the effects of the mass education movement. It began to be recognised that every individual learner is different in his needs and abilities and that he can therefore, for most purposes, learn more effectively as an individual than in a group. The case for individualisation was argued from two main philosophical standpoints, which may be represented by the approaches of Dewey (1916) and Thorndike (1906).

Dewey's argument was essentially humanistic — a concern for the needs and rights of the individual. The purpose of education, in Dewey's view, is to provide an appropriate learning environment in which each student can be helped to make sense of the world in his own way. Thus students should be allowed freedom of choice within the curriculum, rather than being exposed to a teacher-imposed curriculum. An early practical outcome was Kilpatrick's (1921) 'project method', in which each student was given some responsibility for choosing his own area of study, planning his work, obtaining the necessary material, and synthesising it. This method has been rediscovered, extended and widely applied in schools and universities in recent years.

Thorndike's argument, on the other hand, was instrumental — a concern for finding the most efficient method for the instruction of each individual student. The emphasis was on providing students with the opportunity to progress at their own rates, and by different routes, towards teacher-directed goals. This approach received a massive impetus from Skinner's (1954) studies in operant conditioning, which led to early experiments with programmed instruction (Holland and Skinner, 1961), fulfilling Thorndike's (1912) prophetic notion: 'If, by a miracle of mechanical ingenuity, a book could be so arranged that only to him who had done what was directed on page one would page two become visible, and so on, much that now requires personal instruction could be managed in print.' Though it became apparent that the strict Skinnerian approach of linear programming, and even Crowder's innovation of the more flexible 'intrinsic' or 'branched' programming (Crowder, 1960, 1963; Rowntree, 1966) had their limitations, the principles upon which programmed learning was based, such as teaching in small steps and reinforcement of success, have had a profound influence on materials-based learning.

The mainsprings of individualised learning represented by Dewey and Thorndike have fundamentally different philosophical implications. They both, however, require the teacher to provide and organise, in one way or another, a range of learning materials for the students.

The second element in the development of the managerial role has been an increasing recognition that 'learning how to learn' is at least as important, and perhaps more important than learning any given body of knowledge. It is therefore desirable for students, from the earliest stages of education, to begin to experience self-teaching and in this sense to take some responsibility for their own learning. This was implicit in Dewey's philosophy, has been developed explicitly more recently by such writers as Bruner (1967), and relates also to the knowledge explosion of the twentieth century and the need to develop in students the ability to use intelligently the wide range of knowledge sources available. Materials-based learning provides a vehicle for learning how to learn.

Finally, technological developments have extended the range of media through which learning materials may be presented beyond the printed page. The first large-scale use of another medium arose in the Second World War when the need for instruction of a wide range of personnel in the armed services led, especially in the United States, to the extensive use of film, both as a propaganda device and as a didactic tool. The 'teacher as manager' now has at his disposal learning materials presented through a number of different media: printed materials of various kinds, from programmed texts to textbooks; audio materials, including tapes, discs and broadcast radio; video materials, including film, slide, filmstrip and broadcast and closed-circuit television; and computers used in various ways. Two or more media can be combined, as in tape-slide sequences or other more elaborate learning packages.

The need for learning materials offers the teacher another new role: he can be a developer of materials, whether as an individual preparing them solely for his own students' use, or as part of a team preparing them for a wider audience. Many teachers have increasingly accepted this role to a greater or lesser extent since the 1950s, producing materials for their own classes, or taking part in local or national curriculum development projects. They have also adopted for use in their classes materials produced by other teachers, by curriculum development centres of various kinds, and by commercial organisations.

The extent to which such learning materials, rather than the teacher, carry the burden of the total instructional responsibility is very variable. Johnson (1969) has distinguished between instructional *packages*, which provide the teacher with collections of learning materials (perhaps displayed through a variety of media), together with suggested broad strategies for their use, and instructional *programmes*, in which the nature of the materials is such that the detailed tactics for their use are explicitly or implicitly specified.

A simple case of an instructional package would be a textbook which is available to the teacher as a learning resource which may be used in a multitude of ways. A more complex example would be the materials provided by, say, the Humanities Curriculum Project (HCP, 1970), which take the form of resource packs to inform group discussion of important contemporary issues (the educational strategy) but whose precise mode of use (the tactics) can be decided and varied by the teacher, and for which the educational outcomes cannot therefore be precisely specified by the designer of the package. The major burden of educational responsibility in the case of instructional packages is carried by the teacher and in the final analysis the evaluation of their effectiveness can only be conducted at the level of the individual teacher in his classroom. (Grobman (1968) and Schools Council (1973) discuss the evaluation of this type of material as it has developed in the United States and the United Kingdom respectively.)

In the strictest sense, an instructional programme may be defined as:

A vehicle which generates an essentially reproducible sequence of instructional events and accepts responsibility for efficiently accomplishing a specified change from a given range of initial competences or behavioral tendencies to a specified terminal range of competences or behavioral tendencies. (Lumsdaine, 1964)

Programmed texts are the idealised examples of instructional programmes, where the materials carry the full burden of the educational responsibility, and the teacher's role is to set the right student to work on the right programme at the right time. These are often called self-teaching (or self-instructional) materials but, of course, it is really the developer of the materials who is doing the teaching, rather than the student himself. Since their essential feature is the *reproducibility* of the learning they are designed to bring about, it is essential that instructional programmes are evaluated by their developers.

However, these are extreme cases, and the majority of learning materials are designed to carry a major part of the instructional responsibility, but not the whole of it. The conception of what is considered a programme may therefore legitimately be widened to include many types of materials which programmed instruction specialists might reject as 'non-programmes', but for which evaluation by the developer is important and valuable. It is on the improvement of this type of learning materials that this book is focused and some illustrations will perhaps help to define the domain more clearly.

Some Examples of Self-teaching Materials

In the United States especially, quite elaborate projects have been conceived and mounted to explore materials-based learning in schools. Two of the best known of these, both operating at the elementary level, are *Individually Prescribed Instruction* (IPI) and *Program for Learning in Accordance with Needs* (PLAN).

IPI (Lindvall and Bolvin, 1967; Flanagan, 1970) began in 1964 in one elementary school working in co-operation with the Learning Research and Development Center of the University of Pittsburgh. The scheme covers the teaching of the language arts, mathematics and science from the kindergarten class to the sixth year of the elementary school. Batteries of placement tests are used in each subject to identify the level at which each individual student needs to start in each area of each subject. Having identified appropriate starting units for a student, further pre-tests are used to establish what he needs to study within each unit as he begins work on it. On the basis of this information the teacher develops a 'prescription' which lists a certain limited number of exercises on which the student is to work. The appropriate learning materials for that student are then selected from the files. As the student works through the material he encounters exercises covering the material he has just learned by means of which he can check his progress. At the end of each unit there is a post-test to measure the student's mastery of it. Students work largely independently in a large study area seating 50-80 with two or three teachers moving about the room providing individual help when needed and one to three teacher aides who help to score tests and distribute materials. Most of the materials are printed, but audio-tapes are also used (for example to give directions for carrying out simple science experiments).

PLAN (Flanagan, 1967; Shanner, undated) is in many respects similar in principle, though in some ways more ambitious. It was devised in co-operation between the American Institutes for Research and Westinghouse Learning Corporation and first put into practice in 1967 in 14 school districts. On the basis of placement-test data and the interests of the individual student, the teacher and student in consultation establish an agreed programme of studies for the year — a tentative selection of modules in all areas of the curriculum. Each module, or 'teaching-learning unit', consists of a set of directions for the student, the instructional objectives of the module, a list of the learning materials he is to use, what he is to do with them, and sample test items which tell the student how he will know when he has succeeded in achieving the instructional objectives of the module. The student studies the module largely independently and after completing it takes a test, the results of which determine whether he proceeds to the next module prescribed in his programme of studies or is provided with a remedial module.

There are two main differences between PLAN and IPI. The selection of instructional units in PLAN is based on much more information about the pupil — what he knows, how he learns, what his interests are, what his potentials are currently estimated to be, and the long-range plans he is working towards at the time. Also, rather than using specially-prepared learning materials as does IPI, PLAN's modules are assemblages of existing commercial learning materials. Both of these factors make PLAN more flexible and more complicated to administer than IPI, and PLAN is therefore managed by computer. All of the data about the individual students and about the nature of the contents of the modules are recorded on the computer, and end-of-module test scores are fed into it, so that it can then carry out the complex task of selecting appropriate modules to match students' needs.

IPI and PLAN are just two examples of the wide range of materials-based learning which have been used with some success at the elementary school level. They illustrate particularly clearly the complexity of the teacher's managerial role when pupils are learning independently and the importance of the learning materials being demonstrably effective. Such elaborate systems as these have had considerable influence in encouraging much more modest applications of materials-based learning in elementary and secondary schools on both sides of the Atlantic. But such developments have not been confined to the schools. At the other end of the spectrum there have been, especially since the mid-1960s, a number of experiments along parallel lines in university teaching, notably those deriving from the Keller Plan and the Postlethwait audiotutorial method.

The Keller Plan (Keller, 1968; Keller and Sherman, 1974) utilises a sequential set of specially written self-study units pursued by the student at his own pace. The student must demonstrate mastery of a unit by means of a written test before going on to the next unit. The test is immediately marked and problems and errors are discussed with the tutor. If the student fails the test he must study the unit again before taking another test on the same unit. Lectures and demonstrations are used for motivation rather than as sources of essential information, so that the written word, rather than the spoken word, is stressed in teacher-student communication. The Keller Plan was first developed in the context of psychology teaching, but it has been adapted to a number of subject areas (including science, mathematics, engineering and medicine) in a variety of institutions both in the United States and elsewhere (e.g. Green, 1971; Boud *et al.*, 1975).

The Postlethwait audiotutorial approach (Postlethwait *et al.*, 1969) consists of three components. A 'general assembly session' is scheduled for one hour per week for all students. This is followed by an 'independent study session' which involves individual students in audiotutorial study. It can be taken at any time at the student's convenience, and replaces four hours of conventional instruction. Finally, an 'integrated quiz session' for groups of eight students is scheduled for one hour per week. The essence of this method is its combination of group activities with independent work. It has less flexibility than the Keller Plan in self-pacing terms, since the audiotape and materials are changed for each new week's work.

A number of other small-scale uses of materials-based learning in institutions of higher education have been described in the literature (e.g. Haynes *et al.*, 1974; Hills, 1976), some emphasising the use of printed materials as does the Keller Plan, and others incorporating audiovisual materials as in the case of the audiotutorial method, and allowing for varying degrees of self-pacing by students.

A particularly large-scale venture in materials-based learning in higher education in the United Kingdom is the Open University (Perry, 1976), established in 1969 to provide opportunities for adults of disparate backgrounds and abilities to study part-time for degrees in their own homes. At the time of writing the Open University offers over 120 full- and half-credit courses in the fields of the arts, the social sciences, education, mathematics, science and technology, from which students need to accumulate six credits to obtain a bachelor's degree. Each full credit represents approximately 10 to 14 hours of work each week for 32 weeks in the academic year. About 57,000 students are currently enrolled, from whom some 5,800 graduate each year. Each course is divided into learning 'units', 32 for a full credit and 16 for a half credit. A unit is a multimedia learning module, the core of which is a specially-written correspondence text. This may be associated with a variety of other components designed for independent study by the student in his own home — broadcast radio, radiovision and television, tapes, discs, home-experiment kits, readings from set books, offprints and other supplementary printed materials. In addition, there are modest opportunities for face-to-face learning through group tutorials and day schools organised in local study centres and through one-week residential schools organised in the summer vacation. Students are assessed by means of assignments scheduled throughout each course (some marked by tutors and some computer-marked objective tests) and by end-of-course examinations. Similar elaborate systems of materials-based higher education at a distance have been developed elsewhere, notably the Free University of Iran, the Allama Iqbal University in Pakistan and the University of Mid-America.

The above in no sense claims to be a comprehensive review of materials-based learning. No reference is made, for example, to parallel developments in training for industry, commerce or the armed services. It is intended merely to give some indication of the rapid expansion and wide range of learning approaches which depend, to a greater or lesser extent, on the development of self-instructional learning materials.

The Systems Approach to the Development of Learning Materials

Developing effective learning materials is not easy, whether the task involves the preparation of a few worksheets for the use of a single class or whether it involves the design of something as complex as the Open University or PLAN. One response to this problem has been the application to the design of learning materials of the so-called 'systems approach', which can be defined as:

> A point of view which involves taking into account the full complexity of a goal-directed or problem-solving activity — its

starting point, its environmental context, its constraints, its interactions with external features and the interrelationships between its internal components — in developing and assessing alternative solutions. (Johnson, 1970)

Most expositions of the systems approach start with problem identification, and progress through definition of objectives, consideration of alternative approaches to accomplish the objectives, and choice among the alternatives. Its essential feature is that the purpose or goal to be achieved must first be specified and the system designed to achieve that purpose.

The systems approach is not new: it is rooted in such diverse fields as logic, philosophy, communication theory and psychology and represents a synthesis of successful methodologies in problem-solving, planning and development. These elements were first brought together for application in a military context during the Second World War and subsequently transferred to design and planning in industry and commerce. It is only in the last 15 years or so, however, that the systems approach has been successfully applied in an educational context.

This approach to the design of learning materials has been represented schematically by a number of authors at various levels of elaboration: Popham and Baker (1970), Banathy (1968), Tuckman and Edwards (1971), Briggs (1970), Mager and Beach (1967), Thiagarajan *et al.* (1974), and Sedlik (1971) represent a series of increasingly elaborate representations. Tuckman and Edwards' formulation is shown in Figure 1.1.

Other writers, notably those involved with the development of learning materials at various curriculum development centres in the United States, prefer to represent the systems approach in the form of a number of sequential 'stages in product development', often with several 'rules' to apply to each stage. Here again, as in the case of the schematic models discussed above, the different versions are idiosyncratic in their terminology and the extent of their elaboration, even within the output of a single curriculum development centre. For example, several writers have described practices at the Southwest Regional Laboratory for Educational Research and Development: Schutz (1970) divides product development into six stages, and Popham and Baker (197ſ) into seven; Sullivan (1971) describes five separate stages and provides a total of 24 rules within these, whereas Locatis and Smith (1972) identify four stages and 22 rules. Not

Figure 1.1: A Systems Model for Instructional Design (Tuckman and Edwards, 1971)[1]

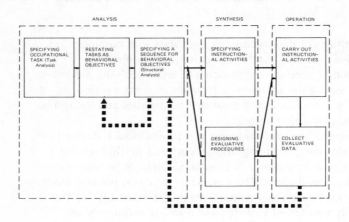

surprisingly, descriptions of practices elsewhere are no less varied (e.g. Borg and Hood, 1968; Flanagan, 1970; Lehmann, 1968; Northwest Regional Educational Laboratory, undated). Figure 1.2 shows one set of such 'rules' for the development of learning materials.

In spite of the great differences in presentation and detail between the representations of the systems approach in Figures 1.1 and 1.2, and indeed between the other descriptions discussed above, there are a number of commonalities between all of these approaches, which are examined in a review by Twelker *et al.* (1972). The following elements are generally present, though not necessarily in this sequence:

1. Problem definition and organisation
   - identification of problem
   - analysis of setting
   - organisation of management
2. Analysis and development
   - identification of objectives
   - specification of methods
   - construction of prototypes
3. Evaluation
   - testing of prototypes
   - analysis of results
   - implementation / recycling.

Figure 1.2: Procedures for the Development of Instructional Programmes (Sullivan, 1971)[2]

Development Stage		Procedures
1. Product formulation	a.	Prepare list of tentative objectives stated in terms of outcomes to be acquired by learners.
	b.	Develop instrument to pre-assess pupil performance on tentative objectives.
	c.	Administer instrument to sample of pupils selected to represent population of learners for whom program is intended.
	d.	Specify program entry behaviors and instructional objectives based upon learner performance on assessment instrument.
	e.	Sequence program objectives (it may frequently be necessary to complete detailed sequencing during Stage 2).
2. Product preparation	a.	List the various components (teacher's manual, storybooks, etc.) of the program and the objective(s) to which each component relates.
	b.	Prepare specifications for the development of each component.
	c.	Develop prototype materials and procedures for each component and field test the prototypes with individual learners and/or small groups.
	d.	Revise the specifications for each component based upon the prototype try-outs.
	e.	Prepare the instructional program according to the revised specifications.
3. Product verification	a.	Specify and arrange try-out conditions approximating those under which the finally developed product will be used.
	b.	Assess the learners on program pre-test measuring performance on each instructional objective.
	c.	Administer the program according to specified try-out conditions.
	d.	Record data during the try-out on transactional and demographic variables (e.g. variations from specified try-out conditions, time spent on various program components, teacher and learner behavior toward each component, class size, learner aptitude) and obtain teacher and learner suggestions for program improvements.
	e.	Post-assess and record learner performance on each instructional objective.
	f.	Release product for general use at this point if performance is high on all objectives. Continue to Stage 4 if it is not.
4. Product revision	a.	Identify objectives on which post-instructional learner performance was low.
	b.	From try-out records identify the transactional and

Figure 1.2 *(contd.)*

Development Stage	Procedures
4. Product revision *(contd.)*	attitudinal factors (see Stage 3-d) related to objectives on which learner performance was low.
	c. Specify all proposed revisions of program objectives and program, including the revisions designed to modify transactional and attitudinal factors related to the low-performance objectives.
	d. Construct final list of revisions based upon the reactions or observed performance with prototypes of revised components) of learners and try-out teachers to proposed revisions.
	e. Prepare specifications for one or more versions of revised program incorporating revisions from final list.
	f. Develop revised version(s) of the program according to specifications.
5. Recycling	a. With the revised version(s) of the program, repeat all events from Stage 3.
	b. With the version of the revised program on which learner performance is highest, repeat all events from Stage 4 if performance is not high on all objectives.

In the context of this book, the most important commonality between all variations of the systems approach is the evaluation element. Prototypical learning materials must be tried out on a sample of students in order to identify weaknesses and discover possible strategies for improvement with a view to making revisions if necessary. In the words of Baker and Alkin (1973): 'At the core of each model, regardless of its complexity of simplicity, regardless of its esotericism or practicality, is the realization and recognition that product development and. . .evaluation are intertwined as snake and staff and that product revision depends upon the generation of. . .evaluation data'; or in the terminology of the systems approach: 'Components which do not function in achieving the systems objectives or which obstruct such achievement trigger modifications in the system to replace or modify the troublesome components. The vehicle for triggering the adaptive response is feedback. . .evaluation is the feedback loop' (Johnson, 1970). In Figure 1.1 this element of the process is represented by the major feedback loop and in Figure 1.2 it occurs mainly within the third development stage, 'product verification'.

The Problem of Terminology

The process of trying out learning materials empirically is described in the literature by many different terms. Some of these, such as 'try-out', 'pre-test', 'rehearsal', 'dry run' and 'field test', are rather informal, and used with corresponding informality (and lack of precision). Others, notably 'developmental testing', 'formative evaluation', 'formative research' and 'learner verification and revision' (LVR), while still often used imprecisely, have acquired a certain status in the educational vocabulary, and it will be useful to discuss their origins and usage at some length.

The term *developmental testing* was first introduced in relation to programmed instruction. Markle (1967) describes three phases during the development of programmes. Developmental testing occurs in the first phase, when the first draft of a programme is tried out on a few students and developed into a workable prototype. The second phase is associated with *validation testing*, in which this prototype is tested on a larger sample of students under carefully controlled conditions. The final phase involves *field testing*, in which the finished programme is tried out in the real classroom situation under widely varying conditions.

The procedures used for developmental testing in the first phase are somewhat variable, but tend to be 'clinical' in the sense that they are the result of close observation of, and often interaction with a few students, singly or in small groups, who may or may not be representative of the target population. Gilbert (1960), in his 'rules for anyone whose foremost concern is the improvement of a given educational subject matter', gives a particularly vivid description of this clinical approach:

> Rule 9. Take your first crude efforts to the student. Remember, he is going to teach you. This student cannot fail. If he doesn't get where you want him to go, you have failed. Try something else. In the absence of anything better, let whim be your guide. If you come to a dead end, vary your approach until you have gotten him where you want him to go. Tape record all sessions. The important thing to remember is to keep varying your behavior until you are successful and to describe what you do. . .

> Rule 12. Take your time. Education has been waiting for you since the dawn of history. When the student has the repertory you wanted

to build, and when you can describe how he got that repertory, you are ready for the next step. Edit the material and try it on another student. Make whatever changes necessary for your program to take care of both students. After fewer than 10 tries, you will have a program which will teach 98 percent of the students. And you will have discovered how to adjust the program for individual differences.

This description also emphasises that developmental testing can begin at a very early stage in the design of learning materials. How early is a matter of some contention. For example, experiments described by Mager (1961; Mager and McCann, 1961) suggested that it is valuable to involve the student even at the stage of sequencing content, which the systems approach requires should precede writing of the instruction itself. Lewis and Pask (1965), however, found that adult learners given freedom to sequence their own learning produced sequences which were grossly inefficient compared with those developed rationally by programmers.

In summary, developmental testing can perhaps most accurately be characterised as trying out early drafts of learning materials iteratively on single students, or perhaps groups of two or three. These cannot be, in view of the numbers involved, representative of the target population in a statistical sense, and may not even be typical of it. The methodology involves face-to-face contact between the developer of the materials and the students while the latter work through the materials.

The term *formative evaluation* was introduced by Scriven (1967), in his now classic paper in which he drew an important distinction between the *goals* of evaluation and the *roles* of evaluation. The goals are the types of questions (in the present context about learning materials) which evaluation attempts to answer. For example, the goal of Markle's (1967) developmental testing is to answer a question such as 'How does this draft programme need to be modified in order that the student can acquire the required knowledge and/or skills?'; the goal of validation testing is to answer the question 'How does the draft programme perform under controlled conditions?'; and the goal of field testing is to answer the question 'How does the programme perform in real classroom conditions?'

The *role* which evaluation has in a particular educational context, Scriven argued, is meaningful only if the goal of evaluation is clear. In the context of curriculum development, he distinguished between a *formative* role and a *summative* role. Formative evaluation is 'the use of systematic evaluation in the process of curriculum construction, teaching, and learning for the purpose of improving any of these three processes' (Bloom *et al.*, 1971). Summative evaluation is the evaluation of the final product of these processes. The role distinction is concerned with who is to use the data collected: 'It is probably more useful to distinguish between [formative] evaluation oriented to developer-author-publisher criteria and standards and [summative] evaluation oriented to consumer-administrator-teacher criteria and standards' (Stake, 1967). Thus developmental testing clearly represents a formative role for evaluation, since the data collected will only be of use to the author/developer of the programme. Validation testing, however, may serve a formative role, if the data are to be used by the author/developer as a basis for further revision. It may also serve a summative role if no further revision is to be undertaken and the intention is to provide a description of the characteristics of the programme which will aid teachers or administrators to decide whether to adopt the programme for use in their classrooms or schools. Similarly, field testing may serve either formative or summative roles. It is important to emphasise that the role evaluation is to serve does not determine the methodology. Scriven (1972) himself contends that a good formative evaluation should simulate a summative one, a point which is illustrated, for example, in Lindvall and Cox's (1970) evaluation of IPI.

Sanders and Cunningham (1973, 1974) have provided an expansion of the concept of formative evaluation as it relates to stages in the development of learning materials using a systems approach. The four stages are described as: (i) pre-developmental activities; (ii) evaluation of objectives; (iii) formative interim evaluation; and (iv) formative product evaluation. These correspond, in Scriven's terms, to different goals which formative evaluation can serve in the development process (though Sanders and Cunningham do not describe them in this way). Such an analysis has been found useful for categorising instruments and strategies for formative evaluation (Lawson, 1974) and also as a model for the evaluation of learning materials (e.g. Krus *et al.*, 1975).

Predevelopmental activities include the identification of educational needs and the establishment of priorities among these identified needs, in order to make decisions on what type of learning materials should be developed.

The evaluation of the developer's objectives is conducted to provide information on their worth so that resources are not invested in developing materials to bring about outcomes of questionable value.

Evaluation of objectives may involve examining the rationale for including each objective, considering the probable consequences of accomplishing it, and investigating its relationship to the priority needs which have been identified. It may also involve collecting the opinions of members of relevant groups (e.g. parents, students, experts of various kinds) on the value of the objectives.

Formative interim evaluation provides feedback to the developer at the stage when he is working with pieces of a product which is not yet fully assembled. This may involve critical appraisal of the materials — by the developer himself and by his immediate colleagues and various outsiders such as specialists in instructional design, experts in the technical aspects of the medium through which the materials will be presented, and teachers who may be using the final materials. It may also involve trying out the draft sections of teaching materials on the students for whom they are intended. The methodology for this may be relatively informal, involving for example the face-to-face interaction with a single student which is characteristic of developmental testing, or it may be more formal, involving groups of students, more or less typical of the target population, working through partial drafts of materials, commenting on them and completing pre- and post-tests.

Formative product evaluation likewise may include critical appraisal and try-out with students, but comes into effect when a more or less complete draft of the educational materials is available. The distinction between interim and product evaluation is not a very clear-cut one. On grounds of cost, for example, it is rarely possible to conduct formative evaluation of learning materials in the final form in which they are to be produced: printed materials are likely to be evaluated in mimeographed form and television or film in a roughcut version since it is usually too expensive to revise the final version in the light of evaluative data. However, two partial distinctions may be made. First, most writers on formative evaluation agree that, whereas in interim evaluation critical appraisal is at least as important as feedback from students, if not more so, in product evaluation it is feedback from students which is the more crucial (a point which will be returned to in Chapter 2). Also, it is at the stage of product evaluation that it is important to try out the materials under realistic field conditions on groups of students that are typical, and if possible statistically representative of the target population.

In summary, formative evaluation is thus very much broader in scope than developmental testing. It can be applied to all kinds of educational (and other) activities as well as to the development of learning materials. In the latter context it includes all the evaluative activities, used at all stages in the development of the materials, which are carried out with a view to improving their quality and effectiveness. It includes collecting data in various ways from single students or groups of students of various sizes, as well as from a variety of other sources, expert and inexpert. These evaluative activities may be carried out by the developer(s) of the materials, or by other persons whose role is specifically concerned with evaluation, or by developer(s) and evaluator(s) together.

The term *formative research* has much in common with formative evaluation. It has been applied mainly in the context of developing audiovisual learning materials, such as films and television programmes. Thus, Palmer (1974), describing the procedures used in the development of *Sesame Street* and *The Electric Company*, defines formative research in terms of systematic audience tests carried out during the course of the production of a television programme in order to evaluate progress towards the achievement of important objectives which have been clearly identified in advance. He describes it as 'eclectic and pragmatic. . .a useful step between basic research and educational practice. . .directly concerned with specific combinations of educational objectives, instructional media, learners, and learning situations'. Like Sanders and Cunningham's (1973, 1974) four-stage conceptualisation of formative evaluation, formative research as described, for example, by Mielke (1974) and Palmer (1972, 1974) is a multi-stage process, serving various goals at the different stages of the development of audiovisual learning materials. One important distinction between formative research and formative evaluation is that the latter can be, and often is conducted by developers themselves, whereas film and television producers do not generally seem to involve themselves directly in evaluative activities. Formative research is therefore not carried out by the developers of the learning materials, but by persons whose role is specifically to conduct research and evaluation. In addition, whereas formative evaluation is generally seen only as a means to improve the product under development, formative research, though having this as its primary function, also looks more consciously towards the possibility of developing generalisable hypotheses for further research and theoretical development.

The most recent term used to describe aspects of the processes used to improve learning materials is *learner verification and revision* (LVR), first introduced by Komoski in hearings before the Select Subcommittee on Education of the United States Congress in the context of the establishment of the National Institute of Education:

> These terms [learner verification and revision] are simply a
> researcher's way of saying that the learning effectiveness of a
> product will be improved if it is taken through a systematic cycle
> of tryouts with learners followed by revisions based on the feedback.
> Such evaluations need not always involve large groups of learners.
> Through appropriate sampling a small group of 'target' students can
> give the product developers ample opportunity to catch errors and
> trouble spots and to revise accordingly. (Quoted in EPIE, 1975)

In subsequent articles Komoski has elaborated this definition. He
emphasises that LVR is 'not a question of proving that materials
instruct, but of proving continuously how well they instruct'
(Komoski, 1974a). This places LVR within the tradition of formative,
rather than summative, evaluation as defined by Scriven (1967), but
equates it not with all aspects and stages of formative evaluation, but
only with that part of formative product evaluation which is concerned
with collecting feedback from students. On the other hand, 'LVR is
not only field test, try-out or other forms of formative evaluation, but
also calls for continuing the gathering of data from learners on both
effective and affective results of a product's use both *before* and *after*
publication, for as long as the product under consideration has "market
life" ' (Komoski, 1974b). This does confuse the issue somewhat. In
Engler's (1976) words: 'What Komoski is doing. . .is throwing out
summative evaluation, replacing it with perpetual formative evaluation,
and calling it "learner verification".'

Figure 1.3 summarises the main distinctions between the terms
developmental testing, formative evaluation, formative research and
learner verification and revision. All are, however, used more loosely
than this in some of the literature. For example, British literature on
the development of audiovisual materials generally uses the term
formative evaluation (e.g. Bates and Gallagher, 1978), formative
research being an essentially American usage. In this book **formative
evaluation** will be used as a collective term to describe all the processes
involved in improving learning materials. The main focus of the book,
however, as expressed in its title, is that part of formative evaluation
which involves the collection, processing and use of feedback from
students. The informal term **student try-out** will be used for this part
of the formative evaluation process. This term is preferred to LVR
because of the connotations the latter has acquired, especially in the

Figure 1.3: Summary of Terminology

Term	Type of learning material	Goal	From whom data collected	By whom data collected
Developmental testing	Programmed texts	To develop a workable programme	Single students (or groups of 2 or 3) not necessarily typical of target population	Developer
Formative evaluation	All	To determine what materials are needed, appropriateness of objectives, effectiveness of partial and/or complete drafts	Experts of various kinds and/or students (singly or in groups of various sizes) not necessarily typical of target population	Developer, or evaluator, or developer and evaluator together
Formative research	Audiovisual	As formative evaluation, and to attempt to formulate generalisable hypotheses	As formative evaluation	Evaluator
Learner verification and revision (LVR)	All	Continuously to improve learning materials, both during their production and subsequently	Students (singly or in groups of various sizes) usually typical of target population	As formative evaluation

United States.

Whereas Markle's (1967) definition of developmental testing and Scriven's (1967) introduction of the term formative evaluation were both directed towards a clearer conceptualisation of the evaluation field, 'learner verification and revision' was introduced to put pressure on the commercial producers of learning materials. This pressure has been partially effective. In 1972 the State of California passed legislation requiring that the process of learner verification be used by all producers of instructional materials wishing to have their materials considered for adoption by the State's elementary schools. In 1974 the

State of Florida also legislated along similar lines, but was a good deal more specific regarding the nature of the LVR process required. The Educational Products Information Exchange (EPIE) Institute (Komoski, 1969), a consumers' organisation for the educational industry, set up a task force in 1974 to produce pilot guidelines for LVR (Tiemann, 1974; EPIE, 1975). Since then, there have been moves towards legislation in a number of American States, including Michigan, Maryland, New Mexico, North Carolina, Texas, and Virginia, as well as in New York City (EPIE, 1976).

Such pressure on the developers of learning materials is not new. Komoski had earlier (1965) pointed out that as few as 40 per cent of the programmed texts then on the market provided evidence of their effectiveness. To remedy this, a Joint Committee on Programmed Instruction and Teaching Machines (1966), under Lumsdaine's chairmanship, prepared a set of technical recommendations for evaluation of programmed materials. In consequence the Journal of Programed Instruction (1966) secured pledges from hundreds of school districts to purchase only those programmed materials that were accompanied by reports of their effects on students. This move was timely, since techniques for the summative evaluation of programmed learning materials were relatively well-established.

In a different context, Title III of the US Elementary and Secondary Education Act of 1965 authorised the birth of government-sponsored agencies to produce properly validated learning materials, but without specifying precisely what validation procedures were to be used. This legislation has had the entirely benign effect of stimulating the staffs of these agencies, and others, to devise and experiment with a whole range of evaluation procedures, both formative and summative.

By contrast, Thiagarajan (1976a) has argued that the LVR pressure movement is both dangerous and premature. It is dangerous because: 'Legislation almost always elicits the minimum level of compliance and replaces intelligent improvements with routine ritual. The undesirable effects of legislating behavioral objectives have failed to teach us a lesson.' It is premature because tried and tested techniques for LVR (or, for that matter, for any of the other elements of the field of formative evaluation) have not yet been established: 'We know next to nothing about the variables which contribute to the efficient collection of useful feedback and their translation into appropriate revisions.' This book aims to contribute to our knowledge of these variables.

Notes

1. Reprinted with permission of Dean Bruce W. Tuckman and Educational Technology Publications Inc.
2. Reprinted with permission of Educational Technology Publications Inc.

2 PRELIMINARY STEPS IN PLANNING TRY-OUT

Many problems remain to be solved concerning formative evaluation in general and student try-out in particular. Baker (1973), Baker and Alkin (1973), Engler (1976), Kandaswamy (undated), Kandaswamy *et al.* (1976), Nathenson and Henderson (1977) and Thiagarajan (1976a), amongst others, have listed some of the critical questions. Central amongst these are the following:

1. What should be the relationship between student try-out and expert appraisal?
2. At what point in the development of learning materials should student try-out be conducted?
3. How many cycles of student try-out and revision are necessary?
4. How many students should be involved in try-out?
5. How should these students be selected and motivated?
6. Who should conduct the evaluation?
7. What types of data should be collected from try-out students?
8. Should data be collected while students are studying the materials or afterwards?
9. How should these data be collected?
10. How can student feedback be translated into appropriate revisions of the materials?
11. Can collecting student feedback and using it to make revisions actually improve the quality of learning materials?

The first six of these questions need to be considered at an early stage in planning student try-out as part of a formative evaluation of learning materials. Each is discussed in turn in the six sections of this chapter, and the key points are summarised at the end of each section. Issues relating to questions 7, 8 and 9 are addressed in Chapters 3 and 5 and the process of translating feedback into revisions (question 10) in Chapter 6. In Chapter 7, the evidence for the utility of the student try-out process is reviewed (question 11), and an experiment to discover the effectiveness of the strategies proposed in Chapters 2-6 is described.

Student Try-out or Expert Appraisal?

There is a certain dichotomy in the evaluation literature between two basically different approaches to the evaluation of learning materials. This dichotomy is encapsulated in Scriven's (1967) distinction between 'intrinsic evaluation' and 'pay-off evaluation', the former involving critical appraisal of the materials by experts of various kinds and the latter proceeding via an examination of the effects of the materials on learners. Lumsdaine (1965) drew a somewhat similar distinction, later elaborated by Cunningham (1973), between 'internal' sources of information, determined by examination of the materials themselves, and 'external' sources, referring to their effects on users. The proponents of pay-off evaluation value external information sources on the grounds that in the final analysis all that counts is the effects of the materials on the learners. This view has found its apogee in the 'learner verification and revision' movement which champions this element of formative evaluation at the expense of the other. It is argued on the other hand, however, that only through intrinsic evaluation and the examination of internal sources of information can important values implied by the learning materials be revealed which pay-off evaluation cannot illuminate.

There have been some attempts to determine experimentally the relative merits of these two approaches. Rothkopf (1963) presented seven alternative programmed texts designed to teach some anthropological information about a fictitious primitive tribe to twelve high school teachers and principals who had just completed a short course on programmed instruction. Each of these 'experts' assigned grades on a six-point scale to each of the programmes, according to how effective they considered they would be in enabling students to score highly on a specified post-test. The actual effectiveness of the seven programmes as measured on the post-test had already been determined using matched groups of students. The correlation between the experts' predictions and observed effectiveness was -0.75.

Rosen (1968) compared two alternative procedures for revising a preliminary version of a television programme on English money. Twenty 'experts' were randomly assigned to two equal groups. The 10 members of one group each devised videotaped supplements to the prerecorded lesson, based on their subjective analyses of its effectiveness in meeting its prespecified goals, while members of the other group devised supplements based on an objective analysis of test data obtained from student try-out of the unrevised programme. The effectiveness of the 20 revisions was tested in sixth-grade classes, using the mean post-test score for each class as a measure of achievement. Pupil achievement across the ten lessons revised using student feedback was significantly better than that across the ten lessons revised by expert appraisal ($p < .025$). Moreover, the lessons revised by expert appraisal were not significantly more effective than the original unrevised programme.

Frase *et al.* (1974) conducted a rather more elaborate experiment on a competency-based kindergarten curriculum unit complete with goals, objectives, activities, teacher materials, pupil materials, teacher guidelines and evaluation items. A panel review board of five primary school teachers (the 'experts') each independently evaluated the unit against predetermined quality checklists. At the same time, a pilot test was conducted in one kindergarten class of 12 pupils, with one teacher delivering the lessons on the unit and another serving as observer to record data on its effectiveness. The teacher and observer spent some time after each lesson making independent notes and then at the end of the unit reviewed and combined their notes and evaluations. Comparing the results of the panel review board and the pilot test, Frase *et al.* noted:

1. That the panel review board was consistently more critical of the unit than the pilot test team;
2. That the panel review board critiques were often not 'therapeutic', focusing on what they perceived to be discrepancies and shortcomings in the content or style of the unit;
3. That many of the problems identified by the panel review board were not manifested in 'real classroom problems' as indicated by the pilot test.

They concluded that 'the panel review board cannot compete with the classroom pilot test data accumulation process'.

Such experiments purport to demonstrate the superiority of data from students over that from experts as a basis for improving learning materials. In fact, however, they do not significantly advance the student try-out *versus* expert appraisal debate, because they fail to take account of the different tasks which experts and students can perform in the process of formative evaluation. The most important distinction here is between tasks related to content and those related to learning effectiveness. The so-called experts used in the above studies were teachers and student teachers. These may be the wrong kind of experts to ask about the potential effectiveness of learning materials because of their biases about the way they believe the content should be taught. On the other hand, there are a number of types of evaluative data, such as information about errors in subject-matter, which the learner is incapable of providing because he does not have the competencies or the knowledge. Markle (1962) has neatly demonstrated that a teaching programme that works, in the sense that it teaches effectively, may be worthless if it is weak in subject-matter content. The programmes used in Rothkopf's (1963) study exemplify just such worthless teaching material.

The distinctive roles of experts and students concerning content and teaching strategy have been examined in some detail in relation to programmed instruction by Lumsdaine (1965) and in relation to learning materials generally by Thiagarajan *et al.* (1974); Thiagarajan, 1976a, 1976b) and Forman *et al.* (1976). They can conveniently be discussed in terms of the matrix represented in Figure 2.1.

Schutz (1970), following the work of Glennan (1967) in a non-educational setting, describes the purpose of formative evaluation in terms of 'reducing uncertainty' during the process of developing learning materials. In the absence of a comprehensive theory of teaching and learning it is never possible to be certain of the effectiveness of learning materials, but the uncertainty can be reduced (though never eliminated) by formative evaluation. The two shaded cells in the matrix in Figure 2.1 represent the types of data which are likely to be most useful in terms of maximal reduction of the developer's uncertainty. Experts are likely to be more helpful than students in relation to content issues, whereas students are likely to be more helpful than experts in relation to issues of 'learnability'. It is not suggested that no useful data can be collected in the modes represented by the unshaded cells in Figure 2.1, but rather that these data are likely to be less uncertainty-reducing, and thus less helpful to the developers of learning materials.

Amongst the questions relating to content which the developer may need to ask, the following would be examples:

Is the material presented theoretically sound?
Are the objectives consonant with the goals of the course?
Are the objectives likely to be attainable?
Is the content important?
Is it treated at a level appropriate to the goals of the course?
Are there any content errors?

Figure 2.1: Expert Appraisal/Student Try-out Matrix

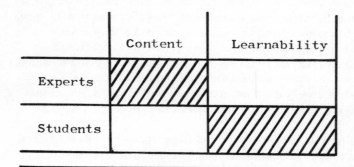

Are the main points adequately developed?
Is the language used suitable for the intended students?
Is the (printed) material free from typographical errors?
Is the technical quality of the (audiovisual) material adequate?
Are the requirements of cost, equipment, space, time, etc.
    appropriate for the intended learning situation?

Issues such as these are most usefully addressed by seeking the opinions of experts at various stages during the development of learning materials. Different kinds of expert will be required to answer different questions: in many cases experts in the particular content area are the only ones who can apply the appropriate judgements, in others it is an editorial function which is required, in yet others the opinions of ·specialists in the technical aspects of particular media (e.g. television, tape-slide) will be most valuable. In organising expert appraisal, it is important to focus each expert's attention towards his own specialist area and away from areas which are not his specialism. For example, it is a waste of the time of a Professor of History to be trying to check spelling and paragraphing, and a waste of a professional editor's time to be trying to check historical facts. Yet such experts will often spend their time in inappropriate ways if an adequate brief is not provided.

In addition to expert opinion, it may be useful to seek student opinion on some questions relating to content, but the data from most students on most of these questions are unlikely to be very reliable (e.g. on matters of content accuracy, or appropriateness of content to level). At best, students are likely to be less efficient than experts in dealing with these issues. At worst, their responses will be idiosyncratic, thus tending to increase, rather than decrease, the developer's uncertainty.

In the case of issues which the developer wishes to resolve relating to the 'learnability' of the materials, the position is reversed. These are issues concerning such questions as how successfully students can accomplish the materials' objectives, whether terms and concepts introduced in the materials are presented at an appropriate level, whether the materials communicate clearly, how long students take to study them, to what extent they follow the learning strategies which the materials prescribe, and what attitudes they express towards the learning experience. Here students, rather than experts, must be the ultimate arbiters. The experts available in this field are described by such terms as 'instructional technologists', 'instructional designers', 'educational technologists' and 'curriculum developers'. The opinions of such experts on draft learning materials can, of course, be of considerable value. This is particularly the case where materials are being produced in a format which has been extensively researched or which is associated with conventions which are generally recognised. For example, much is known about the step size and error rate required in designing programmed instruction (q.v. Markle, 1964), and there are recognised criteria in the design of educational simulation games (q.v. Semmel and Thiagarajan, 1974; Thiagarajan and Stolovitch, 1978). In the more general case, also, an educational technologist with wide experience may be able to provide general guidance on the likelihood of the success or otherwise of draft learning materials. In the final analysis, however, as has been suggested earlier, educational technology can only offer a limited reduction of uncertainty. It is by trying materials out on the students, and collecting feedback from their experiences of them, that the major uncertainty-reduction in learnability will be made possible.

IN SUMMARY

1. Student try-out and expert appraisal serve different subgoals within the overall goal of formative evaluation.
2. Broadly speaking, expert appraisal is more useful in improving content and student try-out in improving learnability.
3. Different kinds of expert may be required to appraise various aspects of draft materials.
4. It is important to brief experts on the particular aspects of draft materials to which their attention should be directed.

When Should Student Feedback be Collected?

Ideally, given the crucial importance of formative evaluation in improving the effectiveness of learning materials, schedules for their development should be planned to allow ample time for evaluation and, in particular, to allow for obtaining and using student feedback. In practice, however, the development of learning materials often takes place within rather tight schedules, predetermined by economic factors, by the availability of staff, or by the necessity of meeting the requirements of the students who will use them. The timing of the collection of student feedback is, therefore, often constrained to a great extent. Given such constraints, there are two competing factors which determine the appropriate time for collecting student feedback: if data are collected too late they may not be able to influence decisions on revision, and if they are collected too early they may be too trivial to consider.

The argument for early try-out is well expressed by Hovland *et al.* (1949), referring to the production of educational films:

> If the evaluations are made when the films are finished products, the most the results can tell the film producer is whether he has succeeded or failed in attaining specified educational objectives. . .
> The stage at which evaluative research would appear to have its greatest potentiality for product improvement is well prior to the completion of a film, when suggestions derived from research can readily be incorporated into the final film production.

Timeliness is therefore of the essence. This point is an obvious one, yet there have been numerous instances of formative evaluation data arriving too late to be usable within the overall production schedule, either because of inadequate planning or, perhaps more frequently, because of excessively ambitious data-collection procedures. Early try-out is advantageous for other reasons also. Many authors are less emotionally committed to their work at early draft stage, and thus more amenable to making substantial changes than at later stages (though on the other hand some authors express a natural reluctance to release early drafts of material, preferring to wait until completely satisfied before submitting their efforts to the tender mercies of students). Also, in the case of elaborate learning materials, and especially those presented through audiovisual media, the cost of revision may escalate rapidly in the later stages of development. For this reason, it is usually necessary to conduct try-out with materials which are at least one step removed from the finished products: thus print will usually be evaluated in the form of typed copy, diagrams may be hand-drawn, pictures may have to be omitted or at least will not be properly positioned or printed, multiple colours may not be available, materials may not be bound, television or films may be presented in the form of a roughcut, etc.

The converse argument for late try-out relates to the principle that the better the quality of the materials being submitted to student evaluation, the more useful and valid are the feedback data. As has been emphasised above, full benefit cannot be gained from student feedback if it is merely viewed as an opportunity to 'clean up' poorly conceived and ill-constructed drafts. Abedor (1972), in his empirical investigations of student try-out, noted that when students found the learning materials disorganised they became frustrated and/or bored and thus became increasingly and excessively hostile, derogatory and vehement in their comments. Also, if drafts have numerous typographical errors, mis-spellings and other editorial faults, students will tend to concentrate on these flagrant errors rather than on the crucial issues of content, style, the development of main concepts, etc. For these reasons it is desirable that review by content and other experts should precede the stage of student try-out aimed at identifying learning problems.

IN SUMMARY

Student try-out should be conducted:

1. After revisions have been made on the basis of expert appraisal;
2. Early enough to enable further revisions to be made on the basis of the data collected; and
3. With as good and complete a draft version of the learning materials as possible.

How Many Cycles of Try-out?

Given that student try-out should occur after expert appraisal and before it is too late to make further revisions, the question remains as to how much data of this kind need to be obtained, i.e. how many cycles of try-out, collection of student feedback and revision are required. One response to this question might be to establish a student performance criterion and to continue iterative try-out and revision until a certain proportion (say, 90 per cent) of a representative group of students meet the criterion. However, this begs a number of difficult questions. First, it is far from easy to determine what constitutes a representative sample of the potential target population. The question of how many students should be used in formative evaluation and in what sense they should be, or can be representative of the target population will be returned to later in this chapter. Secondly, not all materials-based learning is, or can readily be criterion-referenced. Thirdly, as will be seen in Chapter 3, student performance is not the only concern of evaluation.

A number of authors (Kandaswamy, undated; Thiagarajan *et al.*, 1974; Thiagarajan, 1976a, 1976b) have suggested that, following expert appraisal, there should be the following sequence of stages in collecting student feedback, each of which may involve iteration before progression to the next.

1. Individual try-out. The material is tried out on a single student in a 'clinical' setting to identify and eliminate major errors.
2. Group try-out. The material is tried out on a small group of students and data are collected which enable patterns of errors to be identified, their causes to be hypothesised, and revisions to be made which are not based on the possibly idiosyncratic behaviour of a single learner.
3. Field testing. The entire package (consisting of the learning materials and their utilisation procedures) is tested in the conditions for which it has been designed (e.g. in classrooms) without the active participation of the developer or development team. This stage is not expected to lead to substantial revision of the basic learning materials; rather it may lead to modifications to adjunct materials such as a teachers' guide (if the materials are designed to be teacher-mediated) or a study guide (if the materials are intended to be self-instructional).

Baker (1974a) offers a less elaborate model consisting only of stages 2 and 3, again following expert appraisal.

In practice, it is hard to find a single report in the literature of the formative evaluation of a product which has passed through the full three-stage try-out model, though there are quite a number of reports relating to development activities conducted by the larger professional agencies which describe the use of both stages of Baker's model, sometimes with iterations. Thus Nimnicht (1970), recounting the development of the 'basic program plan of education at age three' produced by the Far West Laboratory for Educational Research and

Development, describes two successive phases of group testing followed by field testing. Similarly, Klopfer and Champagne (1975), describing the formative evaluation of the 'individualized science program' conducted at the Learning Research and Development Center of the University of Pittsburgh, mention one phase of group testing followed by two successive phases of field testing. Or again, Jung *et al.* (1971), recounting the development of a 'first year communication skills program' produced by the Southwest Regional Laboratory for Educational Research and Development, describe three successive phases of group testing followed by two successive phases of field testing. Even large development agencies, however, are often satisfied with conducting try-out at only one of the three stages described above. Thus King (1970), describing the development of 'a unit of proof for use in the elementary school' by Wisconsin University Research and Development Center for Cognitive Learning, mentions three successive phases of group testing but no field testing, and Bogatz and Kurfman (1966), describing the development of an 'intra-urban unit for high school geography' by the Educational Testing Service, refer only to a single elaborate field test.

Iterative try-out and revision of draft learning materials is time-consuming and therefore expensive:

> When one balances the effectiveness of systematically developed instruction with its costs, it often may not be warranted. The objectives may not be important enough, or the package may be designed for too limited an audience, or the skills and subject matter to be taught may be so unstable that any instruction developed may rapidly become outdated. Development may only be cost-effective in teaching basic knowledge. (Locatis, 1973)

It does seem self-evident that not all learning materials can justify rigorous, iterative try-out but, as throughout education, the cost-effectiveness judgement is a subjective, rather than an objective one. Although no absolute criteria can be defined, Sedlik (1971) has suggested that materials fulfilling one or more of the following conditions are likely to justify more rather than less extensive formative evaluation efforts:

1. When there is no precedent for either content or teaching method;
2. For more complex and/or expensive learning materials;
3. When the materials seek to change attitudes rather than increase

knowledge;
4. When the materials are designed for long-term rather than one-shot use; and
5. When the target population is large rather than small.

As indicated in Chapter 1, the development of learning materials is often undertaken by individuals and groups who do not have such extensive resources available as do the professional development agencies and whose work is directed towards a much smaller student population. Here the constraints on the extent of student try-out which can be contemplated are much more severe. Abedor (1972) proposed the use of a formative evaluation model involving three successive revision stages (expert appraisal/revise; individual try-out/revise; group try-out/revise) to university and community college teachers from different disciplines who were developing multimedia self-instructional lessons for their students. The model was rejected on the grounds that such iterative development was not feasible for such developers of materials. Time, the high cost of labour and materials, and the difficulty of reorganising multimedia learning packages as a result of even minor revisions were all factors in this rejection. Abedor therefore abandoned this iterative model in favour of a one-shot model involving only group try-out.

Similar problems have been encountered in the development of self-instructional materials at the Open University. In the Open University course design process, as originally conceived (Lewis, 1971), student try-out figured as an important stage. Vigorous efforts were made to implement this principle with the first few courses to be produced (Rowntree, 1971). Unfortunately, however, the operational pressures of the University's first year of course production resulted in only about half of the 32 teaching units of each course being tried out on surrogate students in time for the data to be usable in making revisions before publication, and then not always in the correct sequence. Such operational constraints (in addition to doubts about the legitimacy of some of the data-collection procedures used) led to a somewhat jaundiced view of the usefulness of systematic student try-out (Connors, 1972; Kaye, 1973). As a result, there was a gradual devaluation of the original conception of try-out as an integral part of the course development process to a point where it was being used only intermittently, and somewhat half-heartedly, on a few units of a very few courses. The problem of restoring confidence in the value of formative evaluation in such a context was essentially that of devising a system which could operate effectively within the constraints of an extremely complex course production system and convincing those operating the system that it could be of value. An account of the problems of re-institutionalising student try-out at the Open University is given by Henderson and Nathenson (1977a).

Thus decisions about the timing and extent of collection of student feedback for the purpose of improving learning materials cannot be answered in the abstract or even on the basis of empirical investigation of the relative merits of different strategies in a laboratory setting. They can be determined only in relation to the constraints within which particular developers, or groups of developers of materials are operating.

IN SUMMARY

The extent of student try-out planned will be a function of:

1. The resources available to the developer;
2. The nature of the learning materials under development; and
3. The size of the intended target population.

How Many Try-out Students?

Proposals for procedures to be used in student try-out of learning materials, and descriptions of procedures which have actually been used include sample sizes from a single student to several thousand. This wide range can, however, be conveniently described in terms of three different approaches: the single student or a succession of single students with iterative revisions, small groups of the order of 5 to 50 students, and very large groups of hundreds or even thousands.

The use of a single student or a succession of single students is the *modus operandi* which characterises 'developmental testing' in the original sense of that term as used by Gilbert (1960), Brethower *et al.* (1965), Horn (1964), Markle (1967), etc. It is now sometimes described as 'individual try-out' or 'tutorial-LVR', and has been most commonly used in the development of materials using programmed instruction in the strict sense, for which purpose, as will be seen in Chapter 7, it has been shown to be very effective. Although the use of this type of sample has been suggested for various other forms of learning materials, the only reports of it actually being so used are by Fleming (1963) and Markle (1965) in the script and storyboard stages of the development of educational films. The reasons for this are probably logistical. First, the principal advantage of individual try-out is that it makes possible the exploration of alternative teaching tactics with the student while he is actually studying the material, by inventing them on the spot and trying them out *in situ*. This process is not possible with many teaching media, especially audio or video ones. Secondly, most programmed texts involve rather short study times, or at least can be subdivided into self-contained sections involving short study times, often of no more than an hour or so. An Open University course, on the other hand, involves an average of about 400 hours of student study time (or about 200 hours for a half-credit). Even if the manpower were available to try out materials on this scale in the tutorial mode, it would take many months to work through with a single student, and many years to complete several iterations. This is an extreme case, but the time factor does impose a serious limitation on the utility of this approach. A third limitation relates to the 'believability' of the data from individual try-out. Many developers are worried by the possibility that this method may yield data which are idiosyncratic and atypical of the planned target population. These worries are certainly understandable, and may also be justifiable unless an adequate number of iterations can be performed. It is not easy to put an exact figure on 'adequate' in this context. Gilbert (1960) suggests that 'after fewer than 10 tries, you will have a program which will teach 98 percent of the students', but some practitioners (e.g. Silberman *et al.*, 1964) have found it necessary to use almost three times this many iterations in developing a programmed text.

The majority of student try-out procedures recorded in the literature utilise groups of the order of 5 to 50 students, and are described as 'group try-out' or 'group-LVR'. The most popular figure appears to fall in the range 25 to 40, usually involving a single stage of try-out and revision, but occasionally involving two or three iterations with groups of various sizes (e.g. King, 1970; Jung *et al.*, 1971; Forman *et al.*, 1976). To a great extent, the precise size of the sample appears to depend on operational considerations such as the number that can readily be recruited, the structure of the organisation from within which the recruitment takes place (for learning materials devised for use in schools, for example, a school class is often chosen), and the quantity of data that can conveniently be handled. One factor leading to the choice of larger rather than smaller groups is the expectation of sample attrition. Thus in the Open University it is known that dropout of the order of 25 to 40 per cent occurs on most courses when they are presented to the real student body: a similar order of magnitude can be expected during try-out of a course, and the size of sample is determined with this in mind. In general, more substantial packages of learning materials, involving the commitment of try-out students over many weeks or months may be expected to lead to higher percentage dropout than shorter blocks of material involving only a few hours of study, and the former will therefore imply the necessity of beginning with larger groups of students. The frequency with which group try-out has been employed, with all kinds of different learning materials, suggests that developers, whether intuitively or rationally, tend to place more confidence in the reliability of the resulting data than they do in the individual try-out approach. It is important to recognise, however, that samples in the region of 25 to 40 cannot generally be representative of the target population in a statistical sense: this could only be the case if the target population was an unusually homogeneous one. This does not imply that the developers' confidence in such sample sizes is misplaced. Provided that the students in the sample are typical members of the target population, the aim of student try-out — reduction in uncertainty about the effectiveness of the teaching strategies used — is likely to be achieved and the group try-out approach has, as will be seen in Chapter 7, been shown to be extremely effective with many different types of learning materials.

The use of very large samples is generally associated with the 'field test' type of formative evaluation (e.g. Bogatz and Kurfman, 1966; Jung *et al.*, 1971). It is less commonly described in the literature than group try-out, and then usually as a final stage in formative evaluation following one or more group try-outs. The use of large samples at an early development stage is not justifiable, if only because it would be inappropriate to inflict learning materials at an early stage of their development on a large number of subjects. The advantage of using a very large group is that, using sophisticated sampling methods (for a discussion of which see Moser and Kalton, 1971), the try-out group can be a reliably representative sample of the target population. Greater confidence can then be placed in the data obtained, and the uncertainty factor is reduced to a very low level. The disadvantages are threefold. First, such a large sample will be available only when the materials are being prepared with a very large target population in mind. Secondly, field testing is very expensive and only the largest-scale projects to develop learning materials can afford to budget for it. Thirdly, and most critical, the logistical problems associated with handling the quantity of data involved become horrendous. The data-handling problem can be overcome by the use of a computer, of course, but at the expense of losing the fine-grain open-ended data which are almost always the most useful to the developer in pinpointing exactly the cause of learning problems and in suggesting how the materials should be revised. This is a very serious loss. In any case, even with the aid of a computer, the data-processing time is inevitably increased. Tawney (1973) graphically describes the possible consequences of this in his wry comment on Bruner's (1967) definition of formative evaluation as 'a form of educational intelligence for the guidance of curriculum construction and pedagogy': 'If a military commander demanded the precision of a social survey from his intelligence service, the battle would be lost while the data were still being fed through the computer.'

When writers such as Baker and Alkin (1973), Engler (1976) and Kandaswamy (undated) raise the question of how many learners should be involved in try-out, there is an implication that this question is susceptible to a definitive answer, or possibly a set of alternative answers relating to different types of try-out situation. The research evidence is too limited to provide such answers. Kandaswamy *et al.* (1976) studied the revisions of a short programmed text on a mathematical topic. Two revisers made revisions based on three iterations of an individual try-out method, while another two revisers made revisions based on a single group try-out with 12 students. Each reviser then prepared a further revision using the alternative method. The eight revisions were compared by giving each to a group of 10 learners to study, who afterwards completed a post-test. All eight revisions resulted in significantly higher post-test scores than the original version of the programme ($p < .01$ in all cases). However, there was no significant difference between the four individual try-out revisions and the four group try-out revisions, nor was there any significant difference according to which type of revision the revisers had undertaken first.

Moss and Chapman (undated) compared the feedback on an Open University course from a random sample of 70 students (30 to 35 of whom returned questionnaires) with that from the whole group of 802 students who studied the course in a particular year (80 per cent of whom returned questionnaires). They found very similar patterns of responses from the two groups on study times, difficulty ratings of each section of the course on 5-point scales, etc., suggesting that the feedback from a sample of 30 to 35 could be confidently expected to be reasonably representative of the complete target population.

The present authors, in conducting formative evaluation of Open University courses, have utilised group try-out procedures, with sample sizes normally of 25 to 30, but varying from as few as 12 to as many as 45. The quality of the feedback data and of the resulting revisions does not seem to have been affected by the sizes of the groups used. The variation in group size has been dictated by various factors. Twenty-five to thirty has generally been found convenient, partly because it represents two Open University tutorial groups of the usual size, partly because the logistics of the data-handling can be comfortably managed by one person within the time constraints of the University's course production system, and partly because it is considered (on whatever grounds) to be a satisfactory number by most of the members of Open University course development teams. In cases where smaller or larger groups than this have been used, the reasons have been somewhat idiosyncratic. For example, one course included a summer school as one of its components, and a larger number (45) was considered necessary to simulate adequately this component at the try-out stage. On another occasion, having selected a pilot group of 24, the need arose to conduct some alternative experimental work with half the group, so the formative evaluation feedback group was reduced to 12.

It seems unlikely, at least in the near future, that hard experimental evidence will provide firm guidelines to the formative evaluator on the ideal size of try-out group to use in different situations. Indeed, in view of the wide variety of conditions and constraints under which formative evaluation must be conducted in the context of the development of learning materials, it is doubtful if such prescriptions will ever be possible, or even that they could be of much value to practitioners. The most that can be said is that group try-out with 25 to 30 subjects has not been shown to be inferior to individual try-out or large-scale field test. There is no evidence that larger groups provide more useful data, either in terms of identifying more or different problems in learning the material, or in terms of discovering new solutions. In addition, for most purposes (with the possible exception of formative evaluation of programmed and other short-segment text materials), group try-out has considerable operational advantages. It can also be said that if operational constraints are severe, the group size can probably be reduced to a dozen or so without serious loss of effectiveness. Mathematical models of sampling for student try-out tend to support this view (Burt, 1978). When operational constraints permit, however, two or more iterations with smaller or larger groups may reduce uncertainty about the quality of the final product even further.

IN SUMMARY

1. For most purposes, a try-out group of the order of 25 to 40 students has been found adequate, but groups of 10 to 15 have been used without significant loss of data quality.
2. The main exception to this is in the developmental testing of programmed texts, where iterative individual try-out remains the well-tried technique.
3. Large-scale field testing has more disadvantages than advantages, except as a follow-up to group try-out.
4. The precise size of the try-out group should be determined by · operational constraints, especially: (i) the availability of try-out students; (ii) the expected rate of sample attrition; and (iii) the resources of time and money available to collect and process data.

Selection and Motivation of Try-out Students

In choosing the students who are to comprise a try-out group, the most important consideration is that they are selected from the intended target population. This should be a self-evident principle, but it is all too often violated. The problem then becomes how to select an appropriate sample from among the target population. In some cases, the solution may be dictated by practical considerations. For example, an individual teacher may have only one class available to him on which to try out draft materials, or the policy of the organisation within which materials are being developed may require the use of volunteers on a first-come, first-served basis. Where flexibility has been available, some formative evaluators have attempted to stratify their sample across various demographic variables, and others have stratified on the basis of various intelligence or aptitude tests. Such sampling techniques, however, are always likely to be of questionable statistical validity in view of the small sizes of the samples involved.

If stratification is possible, by far the most important parameter is entry behaviour. Ideally, draft materials should be tried out on students who already possess the appropriate prerequisite knowledge and skills, but who are still naive with respect to the knowledge and skills which the materials have been designed to teach. In most cases, however, it may be expected that some members of the target population will have some prior knowledge or skills in the area with which the learning materials will deal. Pre-testing on the material's objectives of a pool of students from which the try-out sample will be drawn enables a sample with appropriate characteristics of entry behaviour to be selected. It will normally be appropriate for this to consist of a proportion of students with considerable prior knowledge, a proportion with a little, and a proportion with none. However, there may be circumstances in which, for example, it is judged important to select a sample consisting predominantly, or even exclusively of students with absolutely no prior knowledge. Pre-testing is useful not only as a means of selecting a group with predetermined characteristics. It is also valuable even if the sample is predetermined by circumstances and no selection is possible. Knowledge of try-out students' entry level is very helpful in interpreting their individual responses to the materials when the feedback is being examined and decisions about revisions are being made.

One further point about selection of a sample of students for group try-out is worth noting. A number of practitioners in the field have noted that some try-out students have a particular facility for articulating clearly the problems they encounter in studying materials and for proposing revision strategies to overcome them. Some writers (e.g. MacDonald-Ross, 1971) have pointed out how useful it would be if these students could be identified in advance in order to select a potentially rich try-out group. Unfortunately, no methods have been proposed by which preselection of such students might be accomplished. However, some organisations which have a continuing demand for formative evaluation find it useful to maintain a pool of students from which to select try-out groups (see, for example, Forman *et al.*, 1976), and students who have demonstrated this facility could presumably be identified as important members of such a pool. Also, during the analysis of open-ended try-out data, an evaluator soon notices such students and begins to pay particular attention to their responses.

The selection of students for individual try-out is a special case. Scott and Yelon (1969) have argued that, where iterative tutorial sessions are planned, there may be advantages in selecting three different types of try-out student. The first phase might be conducted with a 'subject-matter sophisticate', for example a student who has already done particularly well in the subject concerned, or even a teacher. This will enable such elements as inconsistencies, format errors and unintelligible jargon to be identified which might merely frustrate a typical student. The first phase is thus, in a sense, a form of expert appraisal. The second phase should be conducted with a relatively bright student who, unlike the subject-matter sophisticate, has not mastered the instruction prior to try-out, but is unlikely to be bogged down by many problems. The final phase is the appropriate point to try out the material on a rather dull student. Each of these three phases may involve several test-revision cycles if necessary. Horn (1964) suggests a somewhat similar procedure, using students identified in advance as bright, average and dull (in that order), a precept adopted, for example, in the three-cycle individual try-out part of the experiment conducted by Kandaswamy *et al.* (1976).

A crucial question, which is closely related to the issue of selection of the student sample, is that of what motivates the students to participate in try-out. Gilbert (1960) strongly recommended financial incentives. It is difficult to judge how widespread the practice of paying students to try out prototype materials has been, since most reports of formative evaluation in the literature do not indicate what method of motivation has been used, but it is certainly a popular approach, and probably the most popular. Yet, *prima facie,* cash payment would seem to be a singularly inappropriate form of motivation. The notion that try-out should replicate reality as closely as possible is a basic principle in formative evaluation, and it seems highly unlikely that try-out students who are paid to work through learning materials will behave in the same way towards them as a target population who will not be paid to do so. At the Open University, where early formative evaluation procedures involved paying try-out students, hard evidence has been accumulated which indicates that paid students behave differently. For example, the dropout rate amongst these students was much higher than that amongst real students who subsequently studied the revised version of the same course, and try-out students spent 30 to 50 per cent less time studying the prototype materials than did real students studying the revised materials later.

In general, the motivation for try-out students should be the same as that for the intended target population. It will usually be the case that the target population will study the final learning materials because they wish to learn from them: try-out students should then be selected from volunteers who also wish to learn. In cases where the course being evaluated leads to some form of credit, it is highly desirable that the try-out students should also be studying it for credit. Equally, where the target population of students will be studying under compulsion, it will be appropriate for the try-out students also to study under compulsion — as in the case, for example, of Sulzen's (1972) investigation concerned with military training. In the Open University, the change from paying try-out students to allowing them to study the course for credit has led to a very significant increase in the quality and reliability of the evaluative data. However, it is important to note that, though it is inappropriate to pay try-out students for *studying* the materials, there is no objection to providing them with some tangible recognition of the *additional* work they have to put in to provide feedback data. At the Open University, for example, the course fees of try-out students are remitted, and where set books are prescribed for a course these are provided free.

A further aspect of the principle that try-out should replicate reality as far as possible is providing study conditions for try-out that resemble the intended study conditions for the target population. Thus materials designed for study at home in the evenings should be tried out at home in the evenings, materials for classroom study during school hours should be tried out in classrooms during school hours, etc. This, too, may have implications for the kind (and even number) of students that are selected for try-out.

IN SUMMARY

1. Try-out students should be selected from the target population.
2. If possible, the sample should be stratified on the basis of entry behaviour, determined by pre-testing students on the objectives of the learning material.
3. Try-out students should be motivated in the same way as will be the target population.
4. Try-out conditions should be planned to replicate the study conditions of the target population as closely as possible.

Who Should Conduct Formative Evaluation?

Since 'product development and formative evaluation are intertwined as snake and staff' (Baker and Alkin, 1973), the roles of developer and formative evaluator are of necessity equally intertwined. Most writers on summative evaluation express the view that the evaluator must possess a high measure of independence from those responsible for developing the product being evaluated. This cannot be the case in formative evaluation: developers, evaluators and revisers are necessarily highly dependent upon one another. They can only operate effectively by working as a team, and in the extreme case all three roles can be fulfilled by the same person.

The advantages of a developer conducting his own evaluation are set out by Forman *et al.* (1976) as: (i) he knows what questions he wants to ask; (ii) in face-to-face sessions with try-out students he is in a better position to probe and ask follow-up questions, he is more likely to be sensitive to non-verbal cues, and he can try out on-the-spot modifications; and (iii) cost is kept to a minimum. On the other hand, the same authors point out that the involvement of a separate evaluator has a number of advantages: (i) he has special skills and techniques at his disposal; (ii) he can establish systematic review procedures; (iii) he can record the information collected by evaluation in writing; and (iv) he brings a measure of objectivity to the evaluation.

When the roles of developer and evaluator are separated these two sets of advantages can be combined, provided that close rapport is established between the persons fulfilling the two roles. The present authors' experience has been that the effectiveness of formative evaluation is to a large extent a function of the closeness of communication between the evaluators and the developers in a team producing learning materials. Forman *et al.* (1976) echo this view in their survey of formative evaluation as practised at the University of Mid-America:

> The evaluator cannot simply design a study, collect data, write a report, and give it to the team. If this happens, the team, predictably and understandably, will probably place the study in a desk drawer. The evaluator must work with team members from the start — getting to know their concerns, what types of data they will attend to and what questions are most relevant to them. This is a time consuming and often laborious process, but it is absolutely necessary. No matter what the evaluator does, there is no guarantee that any information will be used, but by working with team members and finding out what *they* want to know, the evaluator can significantly increase the probability that the information will be used.

Palmer (1974) expresses very similar sentiments in his account of the formative research involved in the Children's Television Workshop:

> To the extent that the formative research worked, it worked in large measure because of the attitudes taken toward it by producers and researchers alike. The producers were committed to experimenting with the cyclic process of empirical evaluation and production revision and tended to have the ability not only to see the implications of the research, but also to carry these implications through into the form of new and revised production approaches. . . Moreover, the producers never expected the research to yield full-blown decisions; they recognized that its function was to provide one more source of information among many. From the research

side, because the final responsibility for final production decisions resided with the producers, it was necessary to develop and apply only methods which provided information useful to the producers. Accordingly the producers were involved from the outset in all research planning.

The decision as to who conducts formative evaluation is in practice usually a function of the scale of the materials-development exercise and of the resources of money, time and personnel available. In the kind of large-scale development work represented by the Open University, the University of Mid-America, and the Children's Television Workshop, the amount and type of formative evaluation required demands the full-time attention of persons designated to this particular task, and what then becomes important is the closeness with which these persons work with other members of the development team.

However, much development of learning materials takes place on a more modest scale in which the developer must conduct his own formative evaluation. Here the key factor is providing the developer with the techniques and skills which will enable him to conduct useful and effective formative evaluation and revision. Dick (1968) has shown that untrained revisers behave rather idiosyncratically. He used university students to revise a programmed text in calculus, providing them with the following evaluative data:

1. An item analysis of try-out students' performance on a criterion test;
2. Students' incorrect answers to the criterion test items;
3. A guide indicating where in the programme material relating to each criterion test item was taught;
4. The error rate from each frame of the programme;
5. A sample of students' incorrect answers to programme frames;
6. Try-out students' open-ended comments; and
7. Open-ended comments from expert reviewers and from teachers whose classes had been used to try out the programme.

The revisers reported that frame error rates and the comments of expert reviewers had most influenced their revisions. These are not the data which most experienced professional revisers would regard as most significant and important: 'If Dick's survey of untrained reviser behavior is typical, one realizes how necessary proper training is for those modifying curricular materials' (Popham, 1969a). Certainly individual differences among evaluators and revisers are reflected in the effects of their revisions.

A number of workers have devised and tried out revision 'rules' to assist those revising programmed materials.[1] Baker (1970) asked graduate students in a course on programmed instruction to revise short programmes using a set of revision rules concerned with technical programming issues such as:

A. *When error rates are low and criterion performance poor:*

1. Check to see that the desired behaviors are practiced in the program.

ACTION: ADD PRACTICE

She examined the nature and effectiveness of revisions produced using these rules. Revised programmes were more effective in terms of students' post-test performance than unrevised programmes. However, inspection of the revised programmes indicated that, though the rules as such were generally followed in making revisions, this did not account for the preponderance of stylistic changes. Nevertheless, Baker concluded that 'If such a stable improvement could be predicted across subject matter fields, based on the application of this or a similar set of rules, the impact on educational achievement would be substantial.'

Robinson (1972) developed a self-instructional text, *When Instruction Fails*, which was intended both to teach revision skills and to be used as a practical guide during the revision process. Three groups of student teachers were asked to revise a self-instructional booklet for sixth-grade students concerned with the use of the scientific method in solving problems. One group was given the list of the booklet's objectives, but no evaluative data and no training in revision techniques. The second group was given the objectives and try-out data, but no training in revision techniques. The third group worked through *When Instruction Fails* and was then provided with the objectives and try-out data. Students using revisions prepared by the third group scored significantly higher on the post-test on the problem-solving booklet ($p < .01$) than those using revisions prepared by both groups of untrained revisers. There was no significant difference between revisions prepared by untrained revisers, whether or not they had had access to try-out data.

Similarly, Sulzen (1972) provided infantry school officers with twelve hours of training in revision based on a set of revision rules. The officers then revised programmes concerned with various aspects of military training, presented in audiotape format with multiple-choice questions given on slides. As a result, they were able to produce revisions which were significantly more effective than the original versions.

However, these three studies of training in revision were all concerned with programmed instruction in the strict sense of the term. Abedor (1972) attempted to train university and community college teachers in the conduct of student try-out and revision of materials of a rather more elaborate kind which they had developed for their students. These were self-instructional lessons including slides, tapes, workbooks, models, directions for laboratory exercises, etc. Try-out students worked through the prototype lessons, and completed pre- and post-tests, as well as a questionnaire asking them to rate various aspects of the instruction. The students were then debriefed in a face-to-face session with the author. While the first two lessons by any particular author were being evaluated and revised, Abedor worked alongside him to develop the instruments, to conduct the debriefing, and to design the revisions. For the third lesson, the author was asked to conduct the evaluation and revision himself. By this time the author was found to be competent and confident in developing the instruments and conducting the debriefing, though he still asked for some assistance at the stage of designing revisions. Abedor concluded that this training strategy was a useful one. The present authors have successfully used somewhat similar face-to-face procedures for training university teachers in student try-out and revision of complex multimedia learning packages. Chapters 5 and 6 of this volume represent an attempt to replicate these face-to-face training procedures on paper.

There may be an important side-effect of more people learning and practising the arts of student try-out. Abedor (1972) noticed that the authors he had worked with tended subsequently to produce new lessons that had fewer faults, as revealed by student try-out, than their earlier lessons, and the present authors' experience has been much the same (Nathenson, 1979). It seems that some authors of self-instructional learning materials, like some face-to-face teachers, can use student feedback to make general improvements to their teaching. It may be that: 'Greater sophistication in the tryout phase. . .can lead. . .to the formulation, evaluation, and demonstration of principles which, if applied in the initial preparation of lesson materials, can lead to the need for minimal revision' (Gropper, 1967).

IN SUMMARY

1. Whether the developer conducts his own evaluation or the role of evaluator is designated to another person will be a function of the scale of the operation and the resources available.
2. If the roles of developer and evaluator are separated, the persons fulfilling these roles must work closely together from the beginning of the development process.
3. If the developer is to conduct his own evaluation, he will usually need to acquire some new techniques and skills.

Note

1. Gropper (1975) has provided a particularly elaborate manual attempting to systematise the diagnosis of faults in, and revision of learning materials, but there are no reports as yet of his approach being put into practice.

3 AN INTEGRATED FEEDBACK SYSTEM FOR COLLECTING TRY-OUT DATA

This chapter sets out to describe the integrated feedback system which the authors have evolved for use in student try-out. In constructing any evaluation system, however, there are a number of questions to be considered before tackling the issue of *how* data are to be collected. First, there is the question of *why* an evaluation is to be conducted: the purposes it is to serve. Secondly, there is the question of *what kind* of data are to be collected. And thirdly, there is the question of *when* data should be collected: while students are studying the materials or after they have completed their studies.

In the case of student try-out, the answer to the *why* question is predetermined, since its function is by definition to improve learning materials while they are at a draft stage. The answers to the *what* and *when* questions are less straightforward, and some attention will be given to each of these before turning to the issue of *how* data can be collected, and thus a description of the integrated feedback system.

What Kind of Data?

The last half-century has seen substantive changes in approach to the nature of evaluative data. Historically, the educational evaluation movement developed from the focus of educators on measurement techniques in the 1920s and 1930s, an interest which originated in the need for military selection procedures in the United States during the First World War. The terms *evaluation* and *measurement* were, and often still are used almost interchangeably, especially in the United States. Thus Thorndike and Hagen could write, as late as 1969: 'The term "evaluation" as we use it is closely related to measurement. . . Good measurement techniques provide the solid foundation for sound evaluation.'

The measurement approach to evaluation involves a heavy reliance on scores and other indices that can be manipulated mathematically or statistically. Variables which are unmeasurable tend to be ignored, which imposes a serious limitation on the utility of evaluation: 'This tendency to emphasize the easily measured is a human failure and not a deficiency inherent in evaluation procedures' (Flanagan and Jung, 1970). A second limitation arises from the type of norm or standard against which measurement data are usually interpreted. Most measurement techniques have been developed in a norm-referenced mode, in order to compare the performance of an individual learner with that of a particular reference group. This is the type of norm used, for example, in intelligence tests and also in most public examinations (which are often criticised for precisely this reason). But in formative evaluation it is information about the quality of the learning materials, rather than about the performance of individual learners, which is important: information about the performance of individuals is only useful in so far as it illuminates the effectiveness of the materials. In addition, educational evaluation of any kind inescapably involves sociological or cultural value judgements in the establishment of norms or criteria, whereas the educational measurement specialist aspires to norms which are essentially value-free and antiseptic. Equating evaluation with measurement thus results in a concept of evaluation which is too narrow in focus and too mechanistic in approach.

Superimposed on the well-established tradition of educational measurement, a far-reaching development in evaluation theory was Tyler's (1933, 1942) call for evaluation to be linked with the specification of instructional objectives. Evaluation thus became: 'A systematic process of determining the extent to which educational objectives are achieved' (Gronlund, 1965).

The evaluation-by-objectives model (or goal-oriented model of evaluation) involves a five-stage process:

1. Identification of the objectives to be achieved;
2. Definition of these objectives in terms of the behaviour that would characterise them;
3. Development of appraisal instruments to study this behaviour;
4. Examination of the data gathered in the light of norms by which the adequacy of the behaviour may be judged; and
5. Making final decisions regarding value in relation to the original objectives.

The main focus of the evaluator's task was on the first and second of these stages, in collecting (and uncovering if necessary) the objectives of a programme and, by redefining and expanding them, generating a sufficiently operational set of objectives to make the final three steps of the process virtually automatic.

This evaluation model became pre-eminent in the 1960s. Its primacy dates from the development of taxonomies of educational objectives in behavioural terms, notably those of Bloom (1956) for objectives in the cognitive domain, Krathwohl *et al.* (1964) for the affective domain, and Simpson (1966, 1971) for the psycho-motor domain. Perhaps most influential of all was Mager's (1962) systematic definition of the behavioural objective as one which communicates, explicitly and unambiguously, the teacher's instructional intent. In order to do this, it must describe the learner's terminal behaviour by which its achievement will be recognised, including the conditions under which the behaviour is to occur and the criterion of acceptable performance. Specification of objectives in Mager's terms was intended to operationalise them so that all participants in the teaching/learning process — teacher, students and evaluator — could be perfectly clear both about the goals of a particular instructional unit and about whether, when or to what extent the goals had been achieved.

Determination of congruence between performance and objectives was attractive in the context of the desire for accountability which accompanied the influx of large sums of money from governments and private foundations which occurred as a result of, for example, the establishment of the Schools Council in the UK in 1964 and the Elementary and Secondary Education Act in the USA in 1965. Nevertheless, in spite of vigorous advocacy of the behavioural objectives model of curriculum design and evaluation, notably by Popham (1969b, 1973) and Sullivan (1969), it is now widely accepted that the approach has a number of inherent weaknesses, which have been systematically enumerated in a definitive paper by MacDonald-Ross (1973), and some of which impose serious limitations on the value of the evaluation-by-objectives approach in formative evaluation.

First, not all curriculum developers agree on the desirability of specifying objectives in advance. The usefulness of goals defined in behavioural terms has been most frequently questioned in the humanities disciplines (e.g. Eisner, 1967, 1969; Stenhouse, 1971). Arts subjects, it is argued, are not concerned to reach goals once and for all, but to develop standards of judgement, taste and the critical faculties. The student is expected to become progressively more effective and it is therefore impossible, at any given stage, to specify an appropriate criterion. The evaluator presented with the task of conducting student try-out of learning materials devised by a teacher adopting this philosophical stance will find it difficult, if not impossible, to identify objectives to appraise, may do violence to the teacher's intentions if he does so, and, most importantly, is unlikely to produce recommendations for modifications of the materials which are acceptable to the teacher concerned.

Secondly, even where the teacher who has developed the learning materials is willing (or able) to co-operate in the identification of objectives, their precise definition in operational terms may be difficult or contentious, especially at higher educational levels. The objectives derived are thus normally ambiguous and so, typically, a variety of equally appropriate test items can be written to measure the attainment of any objective. The evaluator's task of developing appraisal instruments to study the student's behaviour after the learning experience is usually, therefore, a much less certain and more contentious matter than the simple evaluation-by-objectives model conceptualises it to be.

Thirdly, application of the evaluation-by-objectives approach in student try-out, though it may be a useful means of locating weaknesses in learning materials, is generally incapable of identifying with any certainty the reasons for such weaknesses or of discovering potential solutions. This problem has been encountered by a number of formative evaluators who have relied heavily on the analysis of performance data, even those who have developed quite elaborate procedures for examining the results of post-tests closely linked to the instructional objectives. Thus Lindvall and Cox (1970), describing the evaluation of IPI, noted that it was impossible to be sure whether poor performance was due to faults in the learning material or, for example, to an invalid test item. They concluded that 'objective data calls attention to a general area of trouble but subjective procedures are necessary to pinpoint the difficulty'. Rahmlow (1971), in evaluating PLAN, found that his analysis of score distributions on individual post-test items could not discriminate between inappropriateness in the instructional objectives and weaknesses in the instruction itself. Nor, assuming the fault lay in the instruction, did the analysis lead to suggestions as to what might be done to overcome the fault. Light and Reynolds (1972) reported similar difficulties when using a quite sophisticated procedure for generating hypotheses to account for failures within an individualised mathematics curriculum and testing them by analysis of post-test data.

However, none of the above is necessarily to argue that the evaluation-by-objectives approach is worthless in formative evaluation. Writers such as Baker and Schutz (1971a) and Sullivan (1971) have rightly stressed the importance of obtaining measures of student performance as part of the try-out process. Certainly, problems arose in early student try-out at the Open University (MacDonald-Ross, 1971) when performance measures were not included at all. In their absence it proved difficult, if not impossible, to place any real value on the responses or comments provided by try-out students. For example, one section of the material might generate frequent comments indicating extreme difficulty, while for another section the comments might indicate relative ease. The immediate reaction would be to recommend alterations to the first section but not to the second. However, performance measures might have shown a high success rate in understanding the first section and total inability to meet the objectives required by the second. Thus performance measures related to objectives are of value, but are not in themselves enough.

A further criticism of the evaluation-by-objectives approach is that in limiting evaluation to a procedure by which outcomes are related to predetermined objectives, it fails to attend to that which occurs in between. The learning material is seen only as a means to an end, and both the content and the learning experiences involved become entirely subservient to goals. This has two undesirable consequences. First, in a learning situation the *process* through which the learning takes place may be extremely important and is certainly inherently interesting. The same goal may often be reached by a variety of means: indeed the means adopted may actually determine the ends which can be attained (Peters, 1959). The means selected for use in a particular situation are therefore a legitimate concern of the evaluator conducting student try-out. Secondly, if the evaluator ignores the process of learning as a consequence of focusing exclusively on the terminal behaviour, he may fail to detect unanticipated side-effects, good and bad.

Two major contributions to evaluation theory which acknowledge the value of the goal-oriented concept but extend it to encourage attention to the educational process are those of Stake (1967) and Stufflebeam (1968; Stufflebeam *et al.*, 1971).

Stake's view is that focus on outcomes has prevented evaluation from taking account of the complex and dynamic nature of the educational process. In addition to *outcome* data, two other bodies of information need to be tapped by the evaluator — *antecedent* and *transaction* data. Antecedents are conditions existing prior to teaching and learning, concerned with the students, the teachers and the learning environment — everything, in fact, which may have a bearing on outcomes. Transactions are all the encounters — of students with learning materials, students with teacher, and student with student — which together comprise the process of education. An important function of any evaluator is to examine the relationships between antecedents, transactions and outcomes in order to seek ways of improving the learning process. For example, during try-out of mathematics worksheets in a primary school class, the evaluator should be concerned with such issues as the try-out students' previous experience of using worksheets (antecedent data) and how often, and for what reasons, they sought personal help from the teacher while using the worksheets (transaction data), in addition to what they learned from the worksheets (outcome data).

Stake also makes an important distinction between recording *intents* and *observations* in the collection of antecedent, transaction and outcome data. He uses the term intents to include objectives in the sense of student outcomes, as well as the teacher's plans for arranging the environmental conditions under which learning will take place, covering the subject-matter, and selecting the teaching methods and media to be used. Intents also include the plans and goals that others have — for example, students, educational administrators and the community at large. Thus the concerns of goal-oriented evaluation are not excluded, but the intended teaching, as well as the intended learning, is included. For example, during the try-out of a computer-assisted learning project the evaluator would wish to know not only the learning objectives to be achieved, but also the teachers' and students' expectations of the project, the administrators' concerns about its potential cost-effectiveness, etc.

Observations are concerned with collecting data on what actually happens, in the present context when learning materials are tried out on students. The evaluator should examine the congruence between intents and observations: the data are congruent if what was intended actually happened. Because the extent of what can be observed is almost limitless, the evaluator needs to restrict the variables to be observed. It is part of his responsibility to rule out observation of those variables which he assumes will not contribute to an understanding of the educational activity. In doing so, he should give primary attention to the teacher's intents, but must also search for unwanted side-effects and incidental gains.

The mainspring of Stufflebeam's concept of evaluation is that it should be: 'The process of delineating, obtaining and providing useful information for judging decision alternatives' (Stufflebeam *et al.*, 1971). Too much educational evaluation, Stufflebeam argues, fails to provide answers to the real questions educators are asking, or at least fails to provide usable answers, or fails to provide answers when they are needed. This aspect of Stufflebeam's contribution to evaluation theory, the emphasis on serving decisions, is highly relevant to formative evaluation. He identified a number of stages in the development of educational systems, including learning materials, at which evaluation can serve the decision-making process. Formative evaluation is involved at what Stufflebeam calls the 'implementation' stage, and student try-out is, in his terminology, a form of 'process evaluation', involving monitoring the way in which the learning materials are used in order to aid the author(s) of the draft materials who have to make decisions about revising them. The process evaluator, in conducting student try-out, focuses whatever evaluative techniques may be appropriate on the most crucial aspects of the learning situation in order to build up an account of what actually happened during the learning process (cf. Stake's emphasis on the collection of transactional data) in order to identify any defects in the design of the materials or in the way in which they have been used.

Recently, other approaches to evaluation have been proposed which, rather than extending the goal-oriented model as did Stake and Stufflebeam, reject it entirely. Notable among these are Scriven's (1971, 1972) concept of goal-free evaluation and Parlett and Hamilton's (1972) illuminative evaluation.

Scriven was concerned that an evaluator might be influenced by knowledge of the goals specified by the designer of learning materials to look for outcomes which are consonant with them. In proposing a goal-free approach he was therefore suggesting that not knowing the designer's goals would encourage the evaluator to be attentive to a wider range of possible outcomes. In this way he was taking the problem of searching for unintended outcomes very much further than Stake's and Stufflebeam's exhortations to the evaluator to 'keep his eyes open'. The goal-free approach is a revolt against the assumption of goal-oriented models that the evaluator must accept that desirable outcomes of an educational programme are relative to what the designer intended. Instead, Scriven is asking evaluators to assess the effects of a programme against the demonstrated needs in the particular area of education addressed by the programme. The feasibility of a pure goal-free approach is questionable, and Scriven admits that it may need to be supplemented by a parallel, but of necessity independent goal-oriented approach. There is no doubt, however, that the notion of goal-free evaluation serves as a useful counterbalance to the predominance of goal-oriented models in the 1960s for anyone involved in planning a data-collection procedure for use in student try-out. It may well be, in fact, that it was this counterbalancing effect which was

Scriven's main intention in proposing the goal-free ideal in the form of a deliberate and slightly tongue-in-cheek over-reaction to the excesses of the goal-oriented school of evaluators.

The task of Parlett and Hamilton's 'illuminative evaluator' is:

> To study the. . .programme; how it operates; how it is influenced by the various educational situations in which it is applied; what those directly concerned regard as its advantages and disadvantages; and how students' intellectual tasks and academic experiences are most affected. [He] aims to discover what it is like to be participating. . .whether as teacher or student. . .In short, [he] seeks to address and illuminate a complex array of questions. (Parlett and Hamilton, 1972)

In essence, illuminative evaluation is designed to take account of the interaction between the *instructional system* and the *learning milieu*. By instructional system is meant the idealised specification of the learning scheme including, for example, a set of pedagogic assumptions, a syllabus, and details of learning materials and their presentation. By learning milieu is meant the social-psychological and physical environment in which students and teachers communicate with one another — a complex network of cultural, social, institutional and psychological variables. Parlett and Hamilton maintain that the goal-oriented approach to evaluation tends to ignore the effect of the learning milieu on the instructional system and vice versa. They acknowledge that the introduction of the instructional system is likely to set off a chain of repercussions in the learning milieu, which in turn will affect the instructional system, changing its form and moderating its impact. The chief concern for illuminative evaluation is to relate changes in the learning milieu to the intellectual experiences of the learner. Parlett and Hamilton describe illuminative evaluation as characteristic of a 'social-anthropological' research paradigm, and their approach has been criticised for precisely this reason, because it tends to view educational processes from a particular social or anthropological perspective, rather than from a broader, multifaceted, educational perspective (Elliott, 1977).

In the context of student try-out it will certainly, in most cases, be impractical to use goal-free or illuminative approaches in their pure forms. Formative evaluation is, after all, a highly action-oriented form of evaluation, in which the aim is to provide information which enables the revision and thus the improvement of educational materials.

However, the contribution that has been made to formative evaluation, as to other forms of evaluation, both by Scriven and by Parlett and Hamilton, perhaps even more clearly than by Stake and Stufflebeam, is a recognition of the importance of selecting and combining a multiplicity of approaches according to the demands of a particular situation. Thus the student try-out of a programmed text designed to teach techniques of statistical correlation might be expected to emphasise a goal-oriented approach (though without neglecting more illuminative data also), whereas the try-out of a project-based course would probably require considerable stress on illuminative or goal-free approaches (but without neglecting some examination of the extent to which the teacher's intents have been achieved).

The above summary of developments in evaluation theory strongly suggests that, in considering what data should be collected in student try-out, attention must be given to the collection of both *outcome* and *process* data. *Outcome* data are required to determine, in performance terms, the extent to which the learning intents have been realised. *Process* data are required to provide information about students' learning experiences as they study the materials, and especially the extent and nature of any learning difficulties they encounter. The present authors have found it helpful to distinguish between five types of process data, relating to issues of *clarity, level, action, attitude* and *time* (cf. Johnson and Johnson, 1970).

1. Data on *clarity* are concerned with such questions as whether the language and style of presentation of the materials is clear, whether students can perceive the relative importance of the various sections of the material, whether any tables or diagrams are clearly presented, etc.
2. Problems of *level* include such questions as whether students with little previous experience of the subject-matter encounter particular difficulties and whether the most able students feel that they have been given the opportunity to pursue the subject-matter at an adequate depth.
3. *Action* data are required to discover what students actually do with the materials. For example, if the materials include self-assessment questions or other types of activity, do students do them? If optional routes are provided through the material, do students use them?
4. Data on *attitude* are concerned with such questions as whether students are motivated by the material, how students feel about

answering self-assessment questions, or engaging in activities, or proceeding through any optional routes which are provided, etc.

5. Data are also required on the *time* students spend studying the materials, including how they distribute their total study time between the various sections or components of the materials. Data on study time have often been neglected in conducting student try-out, but Faw and Waller (1976) have noted that 'empirical evidence. . .suggests that the single most important determinant of how much is learned is probably study time'.

Thus in planning student try-out, it is desirable to devise a feedback system which includes the collection of data focusing on performance, clarity, level, action, attitude and time, a categorisation which will be returned to in Chapter 5.

When are Data Best Collected?

The outcome-process dichotomy is one important dimension of any data-collection system devised for use in student try-out. The second important dimension concerns the time at which data are collected. The basic choice here is between *concurrent* and *retrospective* data collection, i.e. between collecting data while the student is studying or after he has completed his study. It is worth mentioning in passing that this distinction begins to disappear when the learning unit is very small. Thus if one is investigating the success or otherwise of a single page of learning material, such as a worksheet used in a primary or secondary school classroom, the period of study may be so short (say, ten or twenty minutes) that data will in any case be collected at only one point — immediately after the work has been completed. Commonly, however, much larger learning packages are involved in student try-out, requiring many hours of study by the learner, and the retrospective-concurrent distinction is then a real one.

Advocates of individual try-out have approached most closely what might be called pure concurrent data collection, encouraging students to generate an almost continuous stream of data while they are studying. A variety of methods have been used: giving students a general instruction to talk through what they are doing and recording their comments in writing or on tape, using some form of mechanical device which records students' patterns of working through the materials (a technique more commonly used in experimental investigations of reading or of study patterns than in formative evaluation), sitting beside them while they are studying and asking them numerous questions, etc. These methods tend to be costly in terms of the evaluator's time, even when applied to one or two subjects.

What might be called pure retrospective data collection is approached most closely by those who advocate field testing using large representative samples of the target population. The choice of a large sample usually prohibits any methods of concurrent data collection, generally requiring the use of questionnaires after students' studies are completed. These may be written questionnaires, or interviews, or questionnaires administered at a computer terminal.

The relative merits and demerits of concurrent versus retrospective data collection in student try-out, or indeed in other forms of evaluation, have not been adequately investigated. The retrospective method has the inevitable disadvantage that the student may forget important aspects of his experience of learning. There is, of course, much general experimental evidence on the attrition of memory over time, and it is worth noting that forgetting may be both general and selective. Thus there will be an overall loss of detail in the information recalled, but there may also be a greater loss of detail in some areas than in others, due either to the inherent difficulty of remembering certain types of information or to individual students' idiosyncracies. Concurrent data collection is obviously much less subject to information loss in these ways. Small-scale studies conducted at the Open University to compare the use of concurrent questioning and a *post hoc* questionnaire in try-out of the same learning materials with parallel groups of students have indicated that the quality of data collected concurrently is quite substantially higher, in terms of detailed comments and recommendations for revision, than that of data collected retrospectively.

On the other hand, any method of collecting data concurrently will inevitably interfere to some extent with a student's learning processes, so that he learns more effectively, or less effectively, or just differently than if such interference was not occurring. This may raise questions about the validity of concurrent evaluation data which are quite different to those raised in the case of data collected retrospectively. There has been much empirical work on the effectiveness of inserting questions which are deliberately designed to aid learning into learning materials (*vide* Rickards and Denner, 1978, for a recent review). Most of this work indicates that appropriately designed questions can have a specific facilitative effect during the learning process, as well as aiding subsequent retention. It seems at least possible that questions inserted to collect data in student try-out, though not specifically designed to facilitate learning, may, by analogy, have this incidental effect. The limited experimental evidence available, however, suggests that this is not the case. Bank (1972) compared students who had studied programmed materials which included various types of inserted questions seeking evaluative data with students who studied the same materials without inserted questions. The experimental and control groups did not differ significantly in their scores on either a cognitive post-test or on a post-instructional attitude measure. These findings are supported by a further study conducted by Baker and Quellmalz (1972).

Since it is clear that the use of either concurrent or retrospective methods of data collection alone have certain disadvantages, it seems, *prima facie*, desirable to combine both methods, using whichever lends itself to the nature of the particular data required.

An Integrated Feedback System

The integrated feedback system for student try-out which is the central theme of this book involves both outcome and process data collected both concurrently and retrospectively. Four methods of data-collection are involved.

1. The performance of students in assignments, tests or examinations of various kinds provides retrospective outcome data which may be valuable in assessing the effectiveness of the learning materials as well as assessing the students. Such performance measures may exist as an integral part of the learning package being tested, or may have to be specially devised for student try-out, in the form of *post-test feedback questions*.
2. The second method of data collection uses what will be described as *in-text feedback questions*. These are built into the instructional materials at appropriate points, and therefore represent a concurrent method of data collection. They may be linked to objectives and thus be designed to collect outcome data, or they may be concerned with the collection of process data, and thus not linked with objectives.
3. In order to collect process data on students' *study times* a concurrent, rather than a retrospective method has been found to be more reliable.
4. Finally, to complement the concurrent outcome and process data obtained by means of in-text feedback questions, and the retrospective outcome data obtained from integral assessment

exercises and post-test feedback questions, it is sometimes desirable to collect retrospective process data by means of *interviews* with students.

Figure 3.1 summarises these various data-collection procedures on a matrix representing the outcome-process and concurrent-retrospective dimensions. Each of these procedures will now be discussed in rather more detail.

Figure 3.1: An Integrated Feedback System

	Concurrent Data Collection	Retrospective Data Collection
Outcome Data	In-text feedback questions linked to objectives	Integral assessment/ Post-test feedback questions
Process Data	In-text feedback questions not linked to objectives/Records of study time	*Post hoc* interviews

Post-test Feedback Questions

Not all packages of self-instructional learning materials which are to undergo student try-out include some form of student assessment. Most do, however, and it might be assumed that if the students who are to be involved in try-out are required to complete such assessment their performance will enable an adequate judgement to be made by the evaluator of the success or otherwise of the materials in reaching the teacher's objectives. In practice, however, student assessment does not usually cover *all* of the objectives of the learning material, but only samples from the whole domain. Thus, though data from integral assessment may give a general indication of the success or failure of the materials, they may not be sufficiently detailed to pinpoint which part or parts of the instruction, if any, are at fault. As Sanders and Cunningham (1974) point out, it is imperative that some evaluative information be obtained on every objective during try-out. For this reason it will normally be necessary for the evaluator conducting student try-out to devise post-test feedback questions to scrutinise the effectiveness of the teaching in relation to every separate objective.

An example will perhaps illustrate this problem more clearly. An introductory Open University music course is divided into 16 units, involving a total of some 200 hours of study. By the end of the first four units students are expected to be able to achieve two major objectives: to harmonise a cadence in three parts (objective A), and to identify aurally the four basic types of cadence (objective B). These two major objectives are tested by an assignment set at the end of unit 4 (the first assignment of the course) which is marked by a correspondence tutor. During student try-out of the course, it was evident from the performance of the sample of students on this assignment that the two major objectives had not been met. The evaluator who conducted the try-out had anticipated this possibility, and realised that poor performance on the assignment would not necessarily indicate which of the several subobjectives of units 1, 2 and 3 which were prerequisite to the attainment of objectives A and B were the source of the problem.

For example, the objectives of unit 1 included naming of notes on treble and bass staves (sub-objective 1), and writing notes and rests of given time-values (sub-objective 2), both necessary to harmonise cadences on paper (objective A). Other objectives of unit 1, such as distinguishing aurally between higher and lower notes (sub-objective 3) and identifying aurally the number of notes in a chord (sub-objective 4) were prerequisite to identifying cadences aurally (objective B).

In addition, some of the sub-objectives of the earlier units were not sampled at all by the assignment, and performance data from the assignment could give no information about the attainment of these. For example, unit 1 had two further objectives which did not contribute to either of the main objectives A or B, and were thus not tested by the first assignment (sub-objectives 5 and 6).

The relationship between the sub-objectives of unit 1 and the main objectives to be reached by unit 4 and tested in the assignment are shown schematically in Figure 3.2. Similarly, some of the sub-objectives of units 2 and 3 were prerequisite to the main objectives A and B, whereas others were not and were therefore not tested in the assignment.

It is to meet problems of this kind that post-test feedback questions are required in student try-out. The evaluator, with the help of the author of the materials, must devise tests to measure attainment of each sub-objective (in the above instance, one test for each of the four units). Each student is asked to complete the test to the best of his ability when he has done all the work he intends to do on the learning

Figure 3.2: Relationships Between Objectives

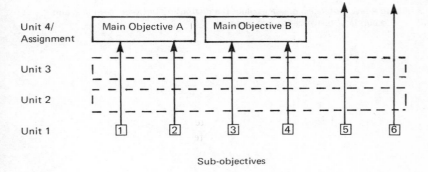

Sub-objectives

materials. He is then asked to look at the answers (which are provided, for example, in a separate sealed envelope) and to check his own answers. He then reports back to the evaluator on a separate sheet whether he got each question right or wrong and, if wrong, what answer he gave. The advantages of this procedure are that it minimises the threat posed to the student by a testing situation and it reduces to a minimum the work required by the evaluator to analyse the results.

In-text Feedback Questions

In-text feedback questions may be regarded as mini-questionnaires integrated into the learning materials. Each one is linked, physically and temporally, to a relatively small section of learning material, ensuring that immediate responses are generated from students. Their function is to invite the student to comment in writing upon the section of instruction he has just completed, in terms of his understanding of the content (i.e. with an outcome orientation) and in terms of his reactions to the learning experience (i.e. with a process orientation). An example of an in-text feedback question with an outcome orientation is given in Figure 3.3, and an example of a series of process-oriented questions in Figure 3.4.

Like any questionnaire, in-text feedback questions benefit from the inclusion of a mixture of types or formats of question. Having decided what information is required, it is necessary to decide what question format is most appropriate to each piece of information. The first step in this decision is the choice between an open-ended and a closed-ended (or precoded) question, each of which has its particular advantages and disadvantages. The principal advantage of closed-ended questions is that

Figure 3.3: An Outcome-oriented In-text Feedback Question

In a few sentences, please explain the distinction between 'primary' and 'secondary' historical source material.

Figure 3.4: A Process-oriented In-text Feedback Question

---

a. Did you attempt the exercise on p.00?   Yes (   )

                                                             No   (   )

b. If not, why not?

c. Whether you attempted the exercise or not, what was your reaction to the author's specimen answer?

---

students' responses are easy to process: a simple matter of counting up the number of responses in each category. By contrast, the processing of responses to open-ended questions is both time-consuming and difficult, involving the careful analysis of a mass of potentially mutually incompatible data for communication to the author of the learning materials. Closed-ended questions have, however, two important disadvantages. First, the effect of asking try-out students to respond to closed-ended questions may be to constrain them unnecessarily and even unhelpfully with the result that they may be prevented from providing a great deal of useful information. Secondly, in order to design an effective set of closed-ended questions, it is usually necessary to collect a sample of typical open-ended responses first and to develop the closed-ended alternatives by content analysis of these. This is not an easy task, and adequate time to carry it out is often not available to the formative evaluator. Open-ended questions suffer from neither of these disadvantages. As MacDonald-Ross (1971) has pointed out, if given the chance to respond in an open-ended way, some students can explicate with admirable clarity the nature of a problem they have encountered, and the whole point of student try-out is to allow them to do so. And while open-ended questions must obviously be carefully devised, they are much less susceptible to minor infelicities of wording than closed-ended ones.

The simplest form of closed-ended item is the dichotomous question which offers respondents only a two-way choice (for example, yes/no, more valuable than/less valuable than, interesting/dull). These are, in general, rather blunt instruments. One extremely useful function of a dichotomous question is, however, as a filter by which only students responding in one way are invited to respond to a subsequent open-ended question. An example of this use appears in Figure 3.4.

Although forcing replies into two extreme categories may sometimes be useful, it is often preferable to add to the two choices one or two more additional alternatives. If the third option represents an intermediate choice (e.g. 'doubtful', 'undecided') the question begins to take on the characteristics of a *scale*, where the respondent is invited to locate himself on some form of continuum. If the third option does not represent an intermediate choice (e.g. 'don't know', 'other, please specify') the question becomes a *list* of discontinuous categories which does not have the characteristics of a scale.

In general, questions involving scales are not of much value in student try-out. There are three reasons for this. First, in a scale such as 'very satisfied', 'satisfied', 'neutral or ambivalent', 'dissatisfied', 'very dissatisfied', no assumptions can be made about the equality of the intervals. Thus 'very satisfied' to 'satisfied' does not necessarily, or even probably represent the same size of increment of intensity as 'satisfied' to 'neutral'. As a result, any attempt to quantify responses in the form of an arithmetic mean is highly suspect. Secondly, even quoting results in the form 'x per cent said very satisfied, y per cent said satisfied, etc.' is not likely to provide information which is of any value in making decisions about how the learning materials should be modified. Thirdly, it has been well-established experimentally that respondents are generally reluctant to use the extreme categories of a scale, so its actual discriminative power is likely to be much less than it appears to be. Occasionally questions involving scales may be useful when it is important to make comparisons between students' responses to different items on the same scale (as in Figure 3.5), but even here the likelihood is small of obtaining information on which to base revisions.

List questions are potentially more useful, though they are difficult to use effectively. An example is given in Figure 3.6. It is probably impossible for any list question to be exhaustive, i.e. to list all the possible responses, and for this reason an 'other' category will almost always be necessary. It is also extremely difficult to devise list questions in which all the items are mutually exclusive. In the question in Figure 3.6 the alternatives are certainly not so, and for this reason students are invited to tick as many or as few alternatives as apply to them. One way round this would be to phrase the question in the form 'At which of the following points during your study did you find your reading of the set book *most valuable*?', but this may be imposing a false choice. Above all, the greatest difficulty in formulating a list question is in deciding which categories to include: if the majority of respondents tick the 'other' category, the question might just as well have been open-ended.

The use of in-text feedback questions to collect both outcome and process data on a concurrent basis is the most crucial, and the most novel element of the integrated feedback system for collecting student try-out data. Chapter 5, therefore, is devoted entirely to the issues of choosing appropriate locations for feedback questions and generating different types of questions to meet the needs of various teaching styles and situations. One final point may be made here, however. No matter how much care the evaluator takes in devising each set of feedback questions to examine students' reactions to a small segment of learning material, he cannot be sure that he has covered all the experiences and concerns which students may have and all the areas in which they might wish to make suggestions. It is therefore highly desirable to include at the end of each set of feedback questions an invitation to students to make additional free comments on the section of materials concerned. Such free comment items are extremely valuable in two respects. First, the comments often contain suggestions of innovative ways to improve the teaching in a section. Abedor (1972), using face-to-face feedback in student try-out, noted that 'students. . .provided strategic level solutions to major instructional problems'. The present

Figure 3.5: A Question Involving a Scale

Please rate each of the five questions you were asked in this section as 'very difficult', 'difficult', 'easy' or 'very easy'. (Tick one box for each question.)

	very difficult	difficult	easy	very easy
Question 1	☐	☐	☐	☐
Question 2	☐	☐	☐	☐
Question 3	☐	☐	☐	☐
Question 4	☐	☐	☐	☐
Question 5	☐	☐	☐	☐

Figure 3.6: A Question Involving a List

How did you tackle the set book? (Please tick one or more of the following as appropriate.)

I read the whole set book before starting work on the study text ☐

I read the whole set book at some point during work on the study text ☐

    (What page had you reached when you did so?) ☐

I read the whole set book after completing work on the study text ☐

I read only the parts of the set book which seemed relevant during my work on the study text ☐

I have not read the set book at all yet but I intend to do so at some future date ☐

I do not intend to read the set book ☐

My way of tackling the set book was different from all the above approaches ☐

    How did you go about it? . . . .
. . . .
. . . .

authors have encountered numerous instances where try-out students' written feedback, especially in response to an invitation to comment freely, not only identifies problems but also provides solutions. Secondly, free comments are an excellent affective measure of students' positive and negative responses, especially of their levels of interest in the learning materials. Such affective responses are very important. In the words of Baker (1974a): 'Even young learners may develop the understanding that instruction can and should be improved and that their own. . .feelings are critical to its success.'

Obtaining Estimates of Study Time

For some types of learning materials, the question of how long students spend studying them may be unimportant. More usually, however, it is of value to obtain an estimate of study time during student try-out. This may be because there is some external constraint on the time students have for study. For example, at the Open University the aim is to subdivide courses into units requiring about 10 to 14 hours of study, since it is necessary for students who are studying part-time to know what commitment of time they are making in enrolling in a course. It is also important to obtain an estimate of study time if a double cycle of formative evaluation is contemplated or if the changes made as a result of a single cycle are to be validated. One needs to know if the changes made as a result of the first cycle have had any substantial effect on the time required by students to study the materials: if the time required is significantly increased, this may have implications for the usefulness of the changes which have been made.

A number of approaches to the estimation of study time have been used by evaluators. One common method is to ask students retrospectively how long they have spent working on the materials, often by means of a closed-ended question in the form of a scale (Figure 3.7). This method has been extensively used at the Open University in *post hoc* evaluation of courses rather than in student try-out. It is generally recognised to give rather unreliable estimates, usually in the direction of substantially underestimating the actual study times. Presumably this is because it is difficult for students to recall, at the end of a period of one or two weeks, the details of what may have been numerous rather short study periods.

Another method which has quite often been used in student try-out is to insert boxes at the beginning and end of major sections of the material, and to instruct students to record the starting and finishing times for each section. This method suffers from two disadvantages.

Figure 3.7: Retrospective Collection of Study Time Data

How many hours have you spent on this unit (including correspondence text, set readings, TV/radio, etc.)?

Under 6 hours	☐
6-8 hours	☐
9-11 hours	☐
12-14 hours	☐
15-17 hours	☐
18-20 hours	☐
21-23 hours	☐
24-26 hours	☐
27-29 hours	☐
30 or more hours	☐
none	☐

First, not all students' study periods will correspond with these major sections: some students will probably split a section between two or more study periods, others will study more than one section at a sitting, and others will back-track for the purposes of revision. Secondly, perhaps because of this lack of correspondence, it has often been found that a high proportion of students forget to fill in the boxes.

The method of recording study times which the present authors have found most reliable in student try-out involves directing students to fill in a simple study diary. This takes the form of a sheet attached to the front of the study text, divided into four columns as in Figure 3.8. Students are asked to record the date, the starting and finishing times of the study period, and the pages or sections of the text studied on each occasion that they study the materials. This approach to the collection of study time data offers a number of advantages.

1. Students rarely seem to forget to complete this type of diary, probably because it is attached to the front of their study text and therefore comes to their attention each time they sit down to study.

2. It makes no demands on students' memories of their study habits and the recording method is designed to match with their actual, rather than some hypothetical, study pattern. It is therefore more likely to provide a reasonably accurate record.
3. It provides information about students' study patterns, as well as about the total time they spend on the materials.
4. If it becomes necessary to examine the time spent on some particular section of the materials, this can generally be inferred from a study of the diaries of all the students.

Figure 3.8: Example of a Study Diary

RECORD OF STUDY TIMES

INSTRUCTIONS: We are very interested in determining the amount of time you take to study each section of this unit. On the Timesheet below, please note the date and time you begin and end your study of each section.

DATE	TIME STARTED	TIME FINISHED	SECTION NO. STUDIED
10·6·77	3·00 p.m.	5·00 p.m.	aims d objectives to 2·2.
11·7·77	7·55 p.m.	9·20 p.m.	Gordon's Chapter 2.
12·7·77	8·00 p.m	9·25 pm	3·0 – 3·3 (INCLUDING EXPER. 1.)
15·7·77	8·00 pm	9·45 pm.	3·4 – 4·2 (INCLUDING EXPER 2.)
16·7·77	8·05 pm	9·45 pm	4·3 – 4·4 (INCLUDING Gordon's 3)
20·7·77	8·00 pm	9·40 pm	5·1 – 5·2 (INCLUDING Gordon't 4)
21·7·77	8·00 pm	10·30 pm	6·1 – 7·3 (INCLUDING Gordon's 5)
22·7·77·	9·00 pm	9·45 pm.	8·1 – 8·2.
23·7·77	12·30 pm	1·15 pm	Gordon's Chapter 8·
23·7·77	8·00 pm	9·30 pm	9·1 – 10·2 (INCLUDING Gordon's 9)
24·7·77·	12·30 pm	1·30 pm	Gordon's Chapter 11
24·7·77	8·00	8·45	Gordon's 10 – 11·2

Post hoc Interviews

Interviews can be a useful mechanism for collecting retrospective process data to supplement the evaluative data provided through the medium of feedback questions. They offer an alternative way for students to express their affective reactions to the learning materials; they give the opportunity to explore in depth problems which have emerged from the analysis of responses to feedback questions; and, most importantly, they permit the exploration of possible solutions to these problems.

In general, when dealing with samples of students of the order of 25 to 30 in student try-out, it has been found most useful to conduct these *post hoc* interviews on a group, rather than individual basis, by means of a discussion with up to about ten participants simultaneously. There has been little systematic study of the relative merits of group versus individual interviewing, but the requirements of collecting data in student try-out do match the advantages which Merton *et al.* (1956) identify as peculiar to the group interview. First, the group interview is economical of the evaluator's time, enabling a wider range of experiences and responses to be uncovered than in a limited number of individual interviews. Secondly, group interaction may serve to remind individuals within the group of details of experience which may otherwise have been forgotten. Thirdly, a single group interview may be potentially richer than a series of individual ones if the interviewer is skilful enough to release the inhibitions of group members so that, as each introduces personal comments, standards are set for others to report progressively personalised comments.

However, the skill of the interviewer is, if anything, even more crucial in group than in individual interviews. Whilst group interviews may serve to release inhibitions, in less skilful hands they may have an inhibiting effect, discouraging individual members of the group from revealing certain attitudes or experiences in what is a relatively public situation. In the words of Markle (1967), 'In a group, a student who would like to ask a "stupid" question may not ask it, fearing that the others might laugh. The "stupid" question may be about some key confusion.' Also, the more articulate members of the group may dominate the less articulate and thus be accorded a certain status as leaders of the group. These leaders may, in addition to monopolising the discussion, influence the reactions of the others in a direction tending to conform to the views of these 'leaders'. In addition, the continuity of group discussion may be interrupted so that a particular topic is not explored in detail, or controversies or discussions arise which are irrelevant to the interests of the evaluator. To avoid these problems, the tone of a group interview must be kept non-threatening and non-intimidating for the students, and all must be encouraged to make a contribution.

The problems of group interviewing are not confined to proper handling of the students. Face-to-face feedback can also be threatening, even devastating to authors of materials. Abedor (1972), who used group interviewing as the main source of data in his try-out model, reported that it was difficult at first for an author to try to understand why students had encountered problems, rather than to defend his materials. But as the students demonstrated how real the problems were to them, they became, through interaction, very real to the author also. The authors with whom Abedor worked had found the expérience somewhat traumatic, though their initial scepticism towards the approach was converted into a firm conviction of the value of the data collected. The degree of trauma experienced by an author in this situation was a function of his tolerance of criticism, the ineffectiveness of the prototype, and his previous experience of such interaction. The authors' experience of involving Open University authors in group interviews strongly supports Abedor's observations.

Nevertheless, in skilled hands the group interview may be a rich source of data in student try-out. It can also be valuable in helping to build a certain *esprit de corps* amongst the try-out team which, after all, includes the students as well as the author and evaluator. Most importantly, face-to-face contact between students and author may help to convince the latter of the desirability of making changes to his draft material. As any formative evaluator knows, his most difficult task is usually to ensure that revisions are made which try-out suggests are desirable. The case study which is presented in Chapter 4 draws attention to this critical revision phase.

4   FROM TRY-OUT TO REVISION: A CASE STUDY

In this chapter, a case study of the complete student try-out procedure is presented. The set of learning materials discussed comprises a full-credit Open University course — the Arts Foundation Course. All Open University students must begin their studies with one of five foundation courses, covering the broad areas of arts, mathematics, science, social science or technology. The original versions of these foundation courses were first presented in 1971/72, and in the last few years these have been replaced by entirely new versions covering the same broad areas.

The original version of the Arts Foundation Course (A100) was presented in each year from 1971 to 1977 inclusive. Preparation of the new version (A101) began in 1975, for first presentation in 1978. Based upon the number of students who studied A100, it is expected that over 40,000 students will study A101 during its lifetime (more than for any other course in the University). The aims of A101 are:

1. To interest and engage students in a study of the unique nature of man in his social context, as expressed through his historical and philosophical thought, religious experiences, literary achievements and artistic and musical creativity:
   (a) examining the different insights, perspectives and methods of historians, philosophers, religious thinkers, creative writers, artists and musicians, leading to
   (b) an integrated study of a single period that illuminates the way in which man's thinking helps to shape his responses to, while at the same time being affected by, the changing material world.
2. Within this framework, to develop the skills of clear and logical thinking, the sensitive evaluation of works of art, and the ability to use primary and secondary source material effectively; also to encourage clear and concise expression of these ideas, arguments and judgements. (Open University, 1978)

The course is organised as a series of blocks of work, each introducing a single discipline (history, literature, philosophy, etc.), but demonstrating inter-relationships of ideas and methodologies with other disciplines. In general, each discipline block contains three units of teaching material, which should take students 10 to 14 hours per week to complete over a three-week period. These discipline blocks lead up to a twelve-unit interdisciplinary block in which the concepts and techniques developed through the preceding blocks are used to study a complex topic, industrialisation in mid-nineteenth-century Britain.

The core of each teaching unit is a specially-written correspondence text, together with one television and one radio programme broadcast by the British Broadcasting Corporation (BBC). Associated with each unit may be readings from set books, assignments, broadcast notes and other supplementary materials of various kinds. In addition, students following the course have the opportunity of attending a weekly group tutorial at a study centre near their home, and are required to attend a one-week residential summer school.

The Planning Phase

Like all Open University courses, A101 was produced by a course team, composed of subject-matter specialists in each of the disciplines involved in the course, educational technologists, editors, graphic designers and BBC television and radio producers. All aspects of course production are the team's collective responsibility (Newey, 1975; Riley, 1975; Mason, 1976; Northcott, 1978). After an early planning phase, responsibilities for the preparation of each course component were allocated to individual members of the course team. Each component then generally went through at least two draft stages, with extensive critical commenting on each draft by other members of the course team, subject-matter experts focusing their attention primarily on content issues, educational technologists primarily on teaching/learning issues, editors and designers on presentation issues, etc.

At a fairly early stage in the planning of the course, the course team made a collective decision to conduct student try-out after these stages of expert appraisal and before publication and presentation to the full student body. A full-credit Open University course is normally studied by students over a ten-month period: with such an extensive and elaborate collection of teaching materials only one cycle of try-out could be contemplated if the period of development of the course were not to be prohibitively increased. Even so, this meant that the writing and expert appraisal stages had to be completed almost a full year before publication in order to conduct try-out in 1977.

The size of the try-out group was also largely dictated by operational constraints. A group of about 45 students was decided upon: this represented two normal Open University tutorial groups, provided a reasonable number on which to pilot the summer school, allowed for the expected dropout (about 50 per cent on foundation courses), and made possible the processing of the required open-ended data by the available manpower.

The try-out system was designed so that students would work through all 32 of the correspondence units, at the rate of one per week, in the form of authors' second drafts which had already been revised in the light of expert appraisal. These try-out drafts were printed by offset litho, whereas the final versions of the units were to be professionally printed. Illustrative musical material, as well as poetry readings, were recorded on cassette tapes, whereas discs were to be used in the published course. Illustrations, especially for the art history units, were provided in the form of separate black-and-white glossy prints: these were eventually to be printed within the correspondence texts. A part-time tutor was employed to provide 40 hours of face-to-face group tuition during the year in study centres and to mark assignments, exactly as would be done in subsequent years. The summer school was organised on a university campus during the summer vacation, again exactly as in normal Open University practice.

In most respects, therefore, the learning components for try-out approximated very closely to those planned for the final course. Two components, however, presented particular difficulties. Production schedules did not permit the final (or pilot) versions of all the broadcast radio and television programmes to be ready for try-out (Bates, 1978; Brown, 1979). This resulted in only about half of the 32 television and radio programmes being tested. Those radio programmes which were available were sent to try-out students on cassettes, instead of being broadcast. The available television programmes, instead of being transmitted nationally, were viewed by try-out students at their local study centres.

It was considered important to select the try-out students from a population resembling as closely as possible the expected student population for the course. It was also necessary for them to live within a limited geographical area, so that they could easily travel to the same study centre for tutorials and to view the television programmes. The sample was therefore chosen from those who had applied to the University to enrol in the Arts Foundation Course in 1977, but whose applications had been too late to secure them a place. Two approximately equal groups were planned, one based on a study centre in London and one on a study centre in Birmingham.

The Conduct of Try-out

All students who had been refused admission to A100 for 1977 and
who lived within a reasonable distance of one of these two study
centres were written to, inviting them to participate in the try-out of
A101. Positive replies were obtained from about 70 students. This gave
only limited possibilities for selecting an appropriate sample. One of
the most significant features of the Open University's student body is
its wide range of educational background (from students who left
school at the age of 14 to those who already have a degree from
another institution). The final group of 45 was therefore chosen to
represent a reasonable spread, deliberately biased to some extent
towards those with weaker backgrounds since a foundation course
must be accessible to these.

The try-out group studied the materials under the same conditions
as Open University students generally, i.e. in their own time at home
(with the exception of the television programmes already mentioned).
Their motivation was also the same. They submitted assignments and
took an end-of-course examination in the usual way, and if their
performance was judged adequate by a formally-constituted
examination board they received a credit for the course. This credit
counted towards their bachelor's degree if they decided to continue
with the University. They were not, however, charged a course fee and
their set books were provided free, as a token 'payment' for the extra
work they were undertaking to provide feedback to the course team.

The evaluator who conducted the try-out programme was one of
the educational technologists on the course team. Data were obtained
using the integrated feedback system described in Chapter 3. The
evaluator asked the author of each unit to indicate those places where
he had concerns about the learnability of his material. For example,
one author wondered whether his introduction, describing how his
unit was structured and indicating how students might tackle it, would
be helpful to students. He was also concerned whether certain
self-assessment questions included in his text would be successful in
helping students to learn the related material. The evaluator then
prepared a set of in-text feedback questions for each unit, based on
the concerns expressed by its author, criticisms made by other members
of the course team, and his own analysis of the material. Between 15
and 20 such feedback questions were prepared for each unit and were
interpolated into the draft text which try-out students were to study.

Responses to these feedback questions were mailed to the evaluator by the students, along with study-time logs and copies of assignments. The evaluator also had the opportunity to explore particular issues further by conducting group interviews with the members of one or other of the two tutorial groups, sometimes with the author present.

Feedback Data and Revision

An examination of how feedback data from one unit of A101 led to revisions will illustrate the try-out system in action. This unit is an introduction to the study of religion. Its major aim is to pose the question 'What is religion?' and to examine various answers which writers on the subject have given. In general, students' responses to the in-text feedback questions indicated considerable problems. They were overwhelmed by the amount and difficulty of the material they had to absorb. Students' performance on the assignment associated with the unit was disappointing in many cases. Study times were, on average, considerably longer than had been intended:

> The mean study time for students works out at *almost 13 hours* for this unit. . .If we also bear in mind the fact that four students failed to return any feedback because the unit was taking them so long that they missed the mailing date, then the mean time is likely to be even higher. The recommended study time for one correspondence unit is 8-9 hours, so students are spending almost twice as long on this unit. . .as they should do. (Mace, 1977)

This quotation, from the section of the evaluator's report which summarised overall student reaction to the unit,[1] sets the scene for the remaining part of this case study, in which the try-out data from one particularly problematical section of the unit will be discussed.

The in-text feedback question shown in Figure 4.1 was presented to try-out students after a section of the unit which, though not amongst the author's principal concerns, was of concern to the evaluator and some other members of the course team. The section began with a question for the students to answer:

> *Can religion be defined?* To set the ball rolling I will ask *you* to give a snap answer to that question. Write down your own definition of religion, or at least a description of how it appears to you, or a list of what you take to be its main characteristics. Some of you may just want to answer, 'Religion is an illusion', or 'a ramp'. But try to say something more than that, and to give some indication of what

is distinctive about religion as an interest, activity, or phenomenon in human history. (Clark, 1977c)

In the discussion immediately following this question, the author explained to students that they probably found it difficult to answer because it is extremely hard to find one definition which encompasses all of the very diverse religious ideas and practices found throughout the world. The unit next asked students to consider 42 different definitions of religion taken from a wide variety of sources. Students were then provided with an exercise inviting them to classify the 42 definitions into categories that seemed to 'belong together'. Following this exercise, the author provided a specimen answer and a discussion in which he classified the 42 definitions into five categories and discussed his reasons for the groupings.

Thirty students returned feedback on this in-text feedback question. The responses to FBQ 3a revealed that most of these students did attempt to define religion as requested by the author. FBQ 3b was designed to elicit students' responses to the author's collection of definitions. They confessed to feeling 'confused', 'bemused' or 'amazed' by the number and range of the definitions they were supposed to take in and make sense of. Several students indicated that this part of the exercise was not relevant to their own attempts at a definition. In response to FBQs 3c and 3d, many students expressed difficulty in understanding the definitions as well as the meanings of various terms and phrases included in the definitions. Figure 4.2 shows those definitions which caused particular difficulty for students and the nature of their problems.

Only half of the try-out students made any attempt to group similar definitions (FBQ 3e) and their answers suggested that many of these attempts were very rudimentary (FBQ 3f). The most common reason given for not attempting to group them was that there were just too many. One student thought that the author's reason for including the definitions was to show how difficult, even impossible, it is to arrive at any conclusions at all. Her comment was supported by many of the other students in the 'Any other comments?' section of the FBQ.

Feedback on the exercise (FBQs 3g-3j) revealed that only one-third of the students made a serious attempt to classify the definitions into categories. Of those who did, nearly all found the exercise too difficult and very time-consuming. Several said they had had to re-read the 42 quotations twice or more in order to attempt a classification and were quite irritated at having to flip back and forth. Nearly two-thirds of

Figure 4.1: In-text Feedback Question from an A101 Religion Unit

---

FBQ 3

3a   Please write your answer to the question on 'defining religion' below.

3b   What was your reaction to the author's discussion (i.e. the 42 definitions)?

3c   Were the definitions clear to you?   ( ) Yes
                                                ( ) No

3d   If not, please say specifically which parts of the definitions were not clear.

3e   Did you try to group together those definitions which appeared to be similar?   ( ) Yes
                                                ( ) No

3f   How did you get on?

3g   Did you attempt the exercise on 'classifying definitions into categories'?   ( ) Yes
                                                ( ) No

3h   What was your reaction to the exercise, the author's 'specimen answer' and the discussion?

3i   Were the 'specimen answer' and the discussion clear to you?   ( ) Yes
                                                ( ) No

3j   If not, please say what was not clear.

3k   What do you think of the author's idea of presenting a 'specimen answer' to the exercise followed by a discussion?

ANY OTHER COMMENTS?

---

the students said that after reading the author's specimen answer and discussion they felt 'muddled', 'confused' and/or 'depressed' since their own answers were so different from the author's.

The response to FBQ 3k was mixed. Some students expressed positive views about the merits of involving students actively in the learning process; others (the majority) felt that this exercise had been too time-consuming; yet others felt that the author's rationale for including the exercise should be made clear. The only new point made under 'Any other comments?' was a suggestion from two students that they should be asked to rewrite their own definition in the light of what they had learned from the 42 definitions and the author's discussion.

After analysing all the data from the in-text feedback questions and elsewhere, the evaluator prepared a written report for the author and other members of the course team concerned with this particular unit. Typically, such a report is in two parts, one dealing with general reactions to the unit, positive and negative, and the other with detailed points, presented section by section. The latter includes a summary of student feedback on each section and, where appropriate, specific suggestions for revision. In the case of the section of the religion unit discussed above, the following suggestions for revision were included in the report:[1]

[1]   *Drastically* reduce the number of definitions presented to students, while maintaining a range. . .If students are to be presented with all the definitions at once then *at the outside* fifteen is as many as they can handle (or three in each group).

[2]   Do not ask students to attempt any grouping of the definitions at this stage. . .It is surely most important that they read and try to understand them first. Instead, encourage students to re-examine their own attempt at a definition in the light of what they have read.

[3]   Explain little-used or 'specialist' vocabulary, or don't use it.

[4]   Omit entirely the exercise. . .Clearly, attempting to categorise the definitions is too difficult, too time-consuming and too depressing a business for most students. . .Having reduced the number of definitions to three in each group, present them *already grouped*. . .Then go on to get them to work out *why* they are so grouped.

[5]   In the specimen answer. . .explain the different approaches more clearly, even at greater length. In general, the level of

language is too high for many students.

[6] It would help students if the definitions were produced on
a detachable card. It would save students all the flipping
backwards and forwards that they find so irritating.
(Mace, 1977)

Figure 4.2: Summary of Data from FBQ 3d in Figure 4.1

Definition number	Number of students (out of 30) expressing difficulty	Nature of the problem
1	5	Meaning of 'the supreme realities of the transcendent order'
4	2	Meaning of 'animism'
6	4	Meaning of 'absolute spiritual reality'
16	11	Hegel's definition unclear
17	6	Meaning of 'sacral sentiments', 'trans-divine' and 'phenomenological'
26	19	Definition unclear
32	12	Definition unclear
33	8	Meaning of 'numinous'
34	15	Definition unclear, especially the term 'dialectic'
36	17	Definition unclear, especially 'empirical reality' and 'supra-empirical'
39	8	Definition unclear

After the author had had time to study the report, a discussion was
held between the author and the evaluator. Face-to-face meetings of
this kind have been helpful in three ways. First, the evaluator is able
to elaborate on certain details in the report which are unclear to the
author. Secondly, the author is able to discuss the recommendations
arising out of the data in greater depth. Thirdly, the evaluator and the
author are able to pursue alternative solutions to some of the problems
thrown up by the feedback data. Thus the evaluator (an educational
technologist on the course team) worked very closely with the
developer of the materials (the author or producer), both in the
critical appraisal stage prior to student try-out and in the try-out
stage itself. It was perhaps because of this close relationship between

evaluator and developer that there were very few occasions (and then usually on minor issues) where the author was not prepared to undertake the revisions which try-out had suggested.

As a result of the try-out of the A101 religion unit, the author made a number of major changes to the text. In the section on definitions of religion, students were again asked to write their own definition, but were now told to keep it by them, amending or amplifying it as they studied the section, and reviewing it after they had completed work on the section (cf. Suggestion 2, p.90). The number of definitions was reduced and they were presented in groups according to the author's categories (Suggestion 1). The exercise was modified in the light of suggestions 4 and 5, as illustrated by the following excerpt from the final version of the unit.

> Out of about a hundred definitions and descriptions of religion that I have collected, I here quote just fifteen for your consideration. I give in brackets the name of the author from whose writings each extract is taken, but the status and authority of the authors is not important for our present purpose. These definitions or descriptions have not been chosen because I think they are the most important, or the most enlightening, or the most intelligible. I have taken them as fairly typical of a much wider range of opinions, and I have grouped them in five groups, each containing three definitions or descriptions relating to religion. As you read them, ask yourself why I have grouped them in this way, and see if you can recognize similarities between the definitions in each group. Afterwards I will suggest an exercise in which you can say what you take to be the common factor or distinctive outlook of each of these five groups of opinions. (Clark, 1978)

With respect to the difficulty students experienced with the language used in the unit (Suggestion 3), the author tried to help the students as much as he could, simplifying his own language to some extent, and adding the following note after the presentation of the 15 definitions:

> No doubt you found that series of quotations somewhat indigestible. They are not free from the off-putting jargon that specialists tend to use. The extracts given under Group C, in particular, may not have been easy to grasp on first reading. (Clark, 1978)

The final suggestion, concerned with putting the definitions on detachable cards, was not taken up by the author.

The Effects of Revision

Final drafts of each component of an Open University course must be approved by the course team before publication. As mentioned above, several members of the A101 course team had had serious reservations about the acceptability of the pre-try-out draft of the introductory religion unit. The final draft, however, incorporating the revisions arising from try-out, was considered entirely acceptable by the whole course team.

The author of this unit was very satisfied with the outcomes of try-out. After receiving the report on try-out, he wrote to the course team chairman:

> I am very grateful for the excellent work which [the evaluation team] have put in on the testing of this Unit, and I certainly wish to take account and advantage of this help in preparing a revised draft for presentation to the Course Team. [The evaluator] has made many detailed suggestions, which will be very helpful to me in such a revision. (Clark, 1977a)

Later, he wrote to the evaluator:

> I can say in general that the feedback provided by the [try-out] of [my] Unit. . .of A101 was useful in many ways, and I should not wish to restrict this usefulness only to the question of 'how to improve that specific unit'. (Clark, 1977b)

This latter comment is interesting in indicating the possible value of try-out as a form of general 'in-service education' for developers of learning materials (*vide* p.57). Letters from authors of other A101 units made a similar point. For example:

> In general [student try-out] goaded me into thinking more carefully about what and how I was teaching. . .With [try-out], since each section of the unit is treated in some detail, there is no relaxing one's efforts. There is no chance of getting off the hook. This added awareness of what one is doing can be applied to any other teaching project. . .Above all, [try-out] prompted me into taking as great a care as I could over the phrasing of questions and answers. And this meant not only thinking of one's own answers to [one's own]

questions but also other approaches to an answer. (Bray, 1978)

And again:

> The main thing I think I learned was the need to be utterly clear
> and unambiguous in my writing; anything that stands any chance
> at all of being misunderstood is sure to be misunderstood by at least
> one student. (Rutter, 1977)

Unfortunately, resources were not available to conduct a study to
validate the revisions which were made to the various components of
A101 as a result of student try-out. No objective data are therefore
available to establish whether the course was improved by try-out and
revision. However, the try-out students had the opportunity of
examining the published version of the course and their unanimous
subjective reaction was that it represented a great improvement on the
version they had studied. The following comment is typical: 'When I
look at the final product of A101 and see what I think are much
improved units. . .I'm really very glad to have taken part. . .Some of
the parts of units which we were quite critical of have been rewritten
to advantage.' Chapter 7 includes a case study of the try-out of another
set of learning materials using the methodology described in this book,
for which objective data on the effectiveness of the revisions were
collected.

Note

   1. The authors are indebted to Dr Francis Clark, the author of the A101 unit
discussed in this chapter, and to Ellie Mace, who conducted the student try-out,
for permission to quote from the evaluation report.

5 PREPARING IN-TEXT FEEDBACK QUESTIONS

The use of in-text feedback questions (FBQs) is the central feature of the approach to student try-out described in Chapter 3. Preparation of effective FBQs is therefore critical to effective try-out. Writing any form of questionnaire is an art rather than a science (Payne, 1951), and in the early stages of evolving FBQs the authors generated them largely intuitively. However, in using FBQs to collect feedback from students on many different types of teaching material, textual and audiovisual, in a wide range of subject-matters (from music and philosophy to systems and mathematics), it has become apparent that some types and formats of question provide data which are useful for revision and some do not. The bulk of this chapter, therefore, presents numerous examples of FBQs which have provided valuable data for revision, each accompanied by a commentary. It has been the authors' experience that, by study of such examples, those wishing to evaluate teaching materials can readily acquire the technique. Before writing FBQs, however, it is necessary to analyse the structure of the teaching material in order to decide what data are to be sought in try-out and the most appropriate points at which to insert FBQs.

Analysis of the Learning Material

Most learning material, presented in any medium, falls into three principal segments, which can conveniently be described as (i) the preliminary organisers, (ii) the main body of learning material, and (iii) the retrospective organisers. The kinds of data required from student try-out on each of these segments are rather different because of their different teaching function, and it is therefore useful to discuss them separately.

Preliminary Organisers

Preliminary organisers are devices used by authors primarily to orient students to what is coming in the main body of teaching material. Five common types of preliminary organiser are: (i) a statement of objectives; (ii) a list of new and/or prerequisite terms; (iii) a concept map; (iv) a study guide; (v) an introduction.

Lists of objectives are perhaps the most common type of preliminary organiser. Their teaching function is to communicate to the student what he is expected to learn from the materials and to indicate what he may expect in assessment material. The task confronting the evaluator is to try to anticipate problems students might encounter when presented with a list of objectives. Process data may be required in all five of the areas discussed in Chapter 3 — on the *clarity* of the objectives, the *level* at which the objectives are written, the *action* that students take when exposed to the objectives, the *attitude* that they hold towards them, and the *time* they spend on them. Figure 5.1 shows three objectives which students are told to read before beginning work on an introductory science text. The evaluator may be concerned that one or more of these objectives are stated in terms that are unfamiliar to some students (clarity). He may also be interested in whether the objectives are pitched at the right level. Another concern may be what students actually do with the objectives (action)? Do they ignore them, read each one carefully, skim them because they plan to return to them at a later time, or what? The evaluator may want to gauge students' attitudes towards the objectives. For example, do students feel it is helpful to be told in advance what they will be learning in this text? Finally, he may want to know how long students spend studying the objectives (time)?

A second type of preliminary organiser is a list of new and prerequisite terms presented at the beginning of the teaching material. Figure 5.2 shows how such a list might be presented. It distinguishes between the terms taken as prerequisites and those developed in the text itself. The prerequisites are further divided into those assumed from general knowledge and those introduced in previous texts. The teaching function of the list of prerequisite terms is to enable students to identify those terms which should be known before studying the text. The teaching function of listing the new terms is to orient students to the main terms they will encounter in the text. The possible mismatch between assumed and actual prerequisite knowledge is one obvious problem facing the evaluator. This is a level problem and the evaluator will want to determine whether the prerequisites assumed from general knowledge and from earlier texts can, in fact, be assumed. There is another potential level problem associated with the list of new terms. Does the list include *all* the terms unfamiliar to students or are other terms introduced in the text which are also unfamiliar to students? The evaluator may wish to ask students to keep a record of any unfamiliar terms they encounter while studying. Action data are required to discover what students do if they find that certain of the general knowledge terms are not familiar, and whether students revise

Figure 5.1: Three Objectives from a Science Text

Objectives

When you have finished your study of this text, you should be able to:

1. Draw flow diagrams or feedback diagrams to illustrate how
physiological systems function or put arrows between boxes to
construct such diagrams;

2. State or recognise at least three differences between the endocrine
and nervous systems as regards their functioning in control and
regulation in the body;

3. Use the principles given in this text to design experiments from listed
data not treated in the text.

---

the terms introduced in earlier texts. With respect to the new terms,
the evaluator may wish to assess the students' attitudes towards the
orienting function of the terms. For example, how do students feel
about being told that a list of new terms will be discussed later in the
text?

Concept maps are a third kind of preliminary organiser. Their
teaching function is to help students to perceive the overall relationships
between the various concepts which will be presented in the main body
of the text. Figure 5.3 shows an example of such a diagram. Once again,
the evaluator's first task is to consider what problems students may
encounter with the diagram. In this case, the most obvious group of
problems may be of clarity. For example, can students visualise the
relationships between the ideas? Is the layout of the diagram clear? Can
students identify the starting and finishing points? Are the reasons for
using different symbols and shadings clear? In addition to feedback on
clarity, data may also be required on level (e.g. Are students familiar
with the terminology used in the diagram?), action (e.g. What do
students actually do with the diagram?), and attitude (e.g. How do they
feel about it?).

The study guide is a fourth type of preliminary organiser commonly
used in self-instructional materials. Its teaching function is to explain
to students how the material is structured and to suggest ways of
tackling it. The evaluator's main concern here will probably be whether
the guide does, in fact, fulfil this function. Are students given a clear
idea about how to study the material? Does it adequately explain how
the various parts of the teaching material are related? If the material is
multimedia, does the guide clearly describe the teaching functions of

Figure 5.2: List of Prerequisite and New Terms

Assumed from general knowledge	Introduced in a previous text	Text No.	Developed in this text	Page No.
acceleration	haemoglobin	14	capillaries	18
inhibition	pH	9	interneuron	24
excitation	habituation	1	synapse	25
etc.	etc.		homeostasis	27
			teleology	27
			etc.	

the various media? Is there any information missing from the guide which the students feel they should be given (e.g. an indication of the most important sections of the material in case they run short of time)? There may also be potential action and attitude problems associated with a study guide.

Finally, there is the type of preliminary organiser which consists of a more discursive introduction preceding the main body of teaching material. Its main teaching function may be to try to motivate students by discussing why the material is relevant and worth studying. In such a case, the evaluator will want to find out whether the introduction does, in fact, motivate the students. Another possible teaching function of an introduction is as a substitute for a formal list of objectives, a study guide or a concept map. The evaluator's concerns will then be much the same as those previously discussed for each of these preliminary organisers.

The above discussion has attempted to be reasonably comprehensive in exemplifying the concerns that an author and/or evaluator may have about preliminary organisers of various types. It is generally not practicable, however, to explore all of these concerns by means of FBQs. To do so would impose an impossible burden on try-out students. It is worth reiterating, therefore, that a critical responsibility of the evaluator, in consultation with the author, is to select those problems which seem likely to be most crucial and to resist the temptation to explore those which may be less important.

In almost every case, it will be appropriate to locate an FBQ immediately after any type of preliminary organiser used in the learning materials. In cases where more than one preliminary organiser is used (e.g. a list of objectives followed by a study guide, or vice versa), two FBQs will normally be required, one after each organiser. Preliminary

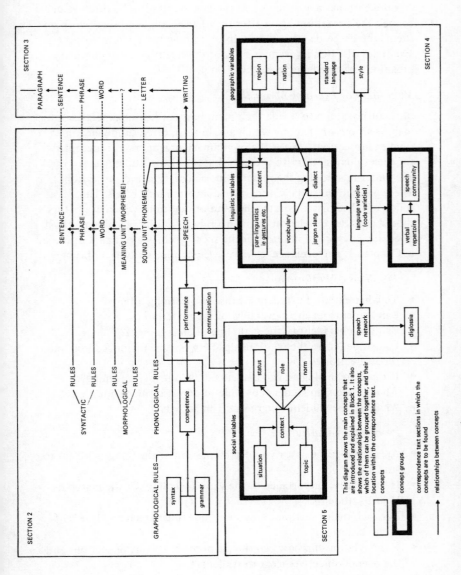

Figure 5.3: Concept Map[1]

organisers are usually intended to be used by students as they work through the materials (e.g. referring back to a concept map as new concepts are introduced). Therefore, in addition to seeking students' reactions to the map at the point they encounter it, it is often valuable to seek their reactions again after they have completed their work on the materials, to discover how helpful it proved to be in retrospect. Examples of FBQs to evaluate each of the five types of preliminary organiser discussed above are given on pp.107-10.

Main Body of Learning Material

Most authors tend to divide their main body of learning material into major sections or chapters which are, in turn, often subdivided into smaller subsections. As for the preliminary organisers, it is necessary for the evaluator to try to predict what problems students may encounter in studying the material in each section and subsection. These predictions will eventually be converted into FBQs. The following checklist illustrates the kind of questions which evaluators should consider in relation to the main body of the teaching material. They are categorised in terms of the six types of try-out data discussed in Chapter 3: performance, clarity, level, action, attitude and time.

Problems of Performance

- To what extent do students realise the learning intents?
- Can students reach an overview of the material?
- Can students identify the main line of an argument?
- Can students see the relationships between the major sections and the subsections?
- If there are analogies, can students draw out their meaning?
- What answers do students provide to self-assessment questions?
- What are the student outcomes to an activity?

Problems of Clarity

- Are the language and style of presentation of the materials clear to students?
- Is the relative importance of the various sections of the materials clear to students?
- For each major section of materials do students have a clear sense of direction?
- Is the relationship between the purposes of the major sections and the overall objectives clear to students?
- Is it clear what students are expected to do with the materials?

- If there are several possible outcomes to an activity, is it clear to students how to evaluate their particular outcome?
- If there are instructions linking one activity to another (e.g. read a chapter from a set book and then return to the text) are students clear about what to do?
- Is it clear to students *why* they are being asked to answer a particular self-assessment question?
- Is the format of each self-assessment question clear to students?
- Is the answer to the question clearly formulated so that students can evaluate the correctness of their own answers?
- If the materials include tables, illustrations, figures, photographs, diagrams, charts or maps, do students find them clearly presented?

Problems of Level

- Are the materials pitched at an appropriate level for students?
- Do students with little previous experience of the subject-matter encounter particular difficulties?
- Can the more able students pursue their studies at an appropriate depth?
- Do students answer self-assessment questions in ways which are not anticipated by the specimen answers?

Problems of Action

- If activities are proposed, do students do them?
- If enrichment activities are offered, do students make any use of them?
- How do students react to self-assessment questions?
- What do students do if they get a self-assessment question wrong?
- If optional routes are provided through the materials, how do students use them?

Problems of Attitude

- Are students motivated by the materials?
- How do students feel about the density of data or ideas in the materials?
- Do students think they have been provided with a sufficient number of examples, or too many, or too few?
- Where examples have been given, do students feel that they illuminate the concept or principle they are meant to illuminate?
- Do students feel that there are adequate opportunities to engage in self-assessment?

- Do students find the self-assessment questions relevant to the objectives or trivial?
- How do students feel about specimen answers which follow self-assessment questions?
- How do students feel about optional routes through the materials?
- Do students see the value of diagrams which are meant to illustrate relevant points?

Problems of Time

- Do students know how much time to devote to the various sections of the materials?
- How much time do students spend on the activities?
- How much time do students spend answering self-assessment questions?
- What is the effect of optional routes through the materials on students' study times?
- How much time do students spend on tables, illustrations, figures, photographs, charts, maps, etc.?
- How much time do students spend looking up the definitions of unfamiliar words or terms?

This checklist is by no means exhaustive, but once again it is sufficiently comprehensive to indicate that it will never be possible for every potential concern to be investigated by means of FBQs. The final decision on what data are to be collected is a matter for negotiation between the author and evaluator. Examples of FBQs to evaluate sections of the main body of teaching materials of different types, presented through various media, are given on pp.111-25.

Deciding where to place FBQs in the main body of teaching materials will be governed primarily by the structure which the author has imposed. A basically discursive teaching text, film, etc. almost always falls into natural sections (whether separated by subheadings, captions, etc. or not). The evaluator will then probably insert an FBQ after each section, since the questions are likely to be meaningful to the students only after they have completed work on the section. However, the essential feature of FBQs is that each must be linked to a relatively small section of learning materials, so that students react to the section while it is still fresh in their minds. The location of FBQs in the main body of the teaching material must also be determined to some extent by the length and conceptual density of its component sections and the evaluator may consider it desirable to subdivide the author's main sections in order to insert more frequent FBQs.

The location of FBQs in teaching materials which set out to involve the student more actively presents rather different problems. For example, if a text includes self-assessment questions the evaluator may want to know whether students bother to answer a particular self-assessment question associated with a section of text: the FBQ could then be placed at the end of the section. On the other hand, the evaluator may be interested in analysing the students' responses to the question in order to determine where students making errors might have gone wrong. Students could then be asked to answer the question in writing at the point when they encounter it in the text. If the evaluator is also interested in obtaining students' reactions to the author's specimen answer or discussion following the question, another FBQ is needed immediately after the author's answer to the self-assessment question. This more complex pattern of FBQs is illustrated diagrammatically in Figure 5.4. Similar, more elaborate FBQ structures may be required to evaluate other kinds of student activity, such as mini-projects, multiple routes through the materials, or when the student is being directed to use a variety of learning components in succession.

Retrospective Organisers

In preparing to write FBQs to evaluate retrospective organisers, as for the other elements of learning materials, the first step is for the evaluator to consider, in consultation with the author, all the possible problems that students may encounter, with a view to focusing on the most critical ones. Authors commonly make use of at least three different kinds of retrospective organisers: (i) a concluding summary; (ii) a checklist of new terms or concepts introduced; and (iii) a self-assessment post-test.

The most frequently used type is probably the concluding summary which usually tries to condense the main points of the teaching material in order to give the student an overview. Some authors also use the summary to list the conclusions which can be drawn from arguments presented in the text. Others include cross-references to the appropriate sections of text where the points raised in the summary are discussed in detail. The main concern of the evaluator is to determine whether the summary fulfils its particular teaching function. This may require obtaining data in all the categories discussed in Chapter 3, but expecially on clarity, action and attitude.

A checklist of new terms or concepts which have been introduced in

Figure 5.4: Location of FBQs to Evaluate Self-assessment Questions

TEXT

Self-assessment question

FBQ — student's answer to question

Author's specimen answer

FBQ — student's reaction to specimen answer

TEXT
CONTINUES

the materials is essentially an access device to help students remind themselves of the meanings of these terms or concepts. The checklist thus supplements the introduction of the term in its appropriate context in the main body of the material, and enables students to revise or review without going through all of the materials again. The evaluator's most obvious concern will be whether the checklist is sufficiently comprehensive. Can students identify any additional terms or concepts from the text which have not been included in the checklist? The evaluator may also wish to know how students use the checklist and whether they consider it to be a helpful aid to learning.

Self-assessment post-tests are sometimes provided at the end of learning materials to enable students to assess their understanding of the teaching material and thus to diagnose their own strengths and weaknesses. Here the evaluator's first concern will probably be the clarity of the post-test questions. Is there any ambiguity? Does any of the terminology in the questions confuse students? Similarly, are the author's specimen answers to the post-test clear? Action data may also be important. What use do students make of the post-test? What do they do if their answers are different from the author's? The evaluator may also want to analyse students' answers (performance data).

The positioning of FBQs to evaluate retrospective organisers is straightforward: it is usually sufficient to locate one FBQ after the summary, after the checklist, or after the self-assessment post-test. Examples of FBQs on retrospective organisers are given on pp. 127-8.

Writing Feedback Questions

In this section of the chapter, a number of examples of in-text feedback questions will be presented, together with a commentary on each. For convenience, these will be grouped according to whether they are designed to evaluate preliminary organisers, the main body of teaching material, or retrospective organisers. They have been used in student try-out of learning materials in various subject areas presented through various media, and have provided data which have been valuable in the revision of these materials. However, it must be remembered that each one was written to explore the concerns which a particular evaluator identified (usually in consultation with an author) about a specific piece of learning material. These FBQs are not therefore offered as idealised models, but to exemplify the approach to this methodology for student try-out.

FBQs on Preliminary Organisers

Figure 5.5 is an example of an FBQ designed to evaluate a list of
objectives at the beginning of a self-instructional chemistry text.
FBQ 1a is designed to discover what students actually do with the list
(action data). Being concerned that some students might not
understand the meaning of a completely open-ended question such as
'What did you do with the objectives for this unit?', the evaluator
includes some prompting cues to help focus the students' responses.
FBQ 1b (time data) enables the evaluator to compare students' actions
as indicated in 1a with the time they spent on this task. Question 1c
seeks attitude data about students' feelings towards the objectives. It
follows the same prompting pattern as 1a. In 1d, the evaluator is
interested in clarity and chooses a closed-ended 'yes/no' question to
act as a filter for the open-ended question 1e. Only those students who
have difficulty understanding the meaning of any of the objectives and
therefore answer 'yes' to 1d also answer 1e. FBQ 1f asks students rather
bluntly whether the objectives have been a helpful aid to learning at
this early stage. It is often interesting to compare students' responses
to an FBQ like 1f with their responses to a similar FBQ asked after
they have completed the material. The 'Any Other Comments?' item
at the end of the FBQ allows students complete freedom to react to
the objectives. In practice, this item is extensively used by students in
a variety of ways. Some students, for example, use it to suggest ways
in which the use of objectives as a teaching aid can be improved: e.g.
'They would mean more if integrated at strategic points in the text,
and reproduced at the *end* of the text.'

FBQ 2 in Figure 5.6 was used to evaluate the list of six prerequisite
terms, part of which is given in Figure 5.2. The evaluator is trying to
find out whether students' entry levels are adequate to define those
terms which the author assumes as prerequisites. It is generally more
useful to frame questions like 2a and 2c in a way which requires
students to write their definitions, rather than asking them whether
they understand the terms. The danger with the latter is that students
may think they understand the terms when, in practice, they do not.
Questions 2b and 2d are to determine what course of action students
pursued if they could not define the terms.

FBQ 3 (Figure 5.7) is to elicit student reaction to the concept map
shown in Figure 5.3 which was provided as a preliminary organiser to a
correspondence text for students of education. Question 3a seeks data
on how students thought the map should be used (action), and question
3b on students' attitudes to the presentation of this form of preliminary

Figure 5.5: FBQ on Objectives in a Chemistry Text[2]

FBQ 1

1a   What did you *do* with the objectives for this text? (Did you ignore
      them, read them rather quickly, read them more than once, study
      each one carefully, make a précis of them, or what?)

1b   Approximately how long did you spend on the objectives?
                  (   ) minutes

1c   Did the objectives make you want to get into the subject-matter,
      put you off, or what?

1d   Did you have any difficulty in understanding what is meant by any
      of the objectives?
                  Yes   (   )
                  No   (   )

1e   If yes, please specify.

1f   One of the reasons for including a list of objectives at the beginning
      of a text is to tell students in advance what they are expected to
      learn in the text. Have you found the objectives in this text helpful
      in this respect?
                  Yes   (   )
                  No   (   )
      Please explain your answer

ANY OTHER COMMENTS?

---

organiser. The remaining questions (3c-3e) are designed to discover how
clear various aspects of the map were to students.

FBQ 4 in Figure 5.8 is a feedback question which could be used, in
a modified form, to evaluate any study guide. Questions 4a and 4b are
designed to assess the clarity of the guide, 4a acting as a filter to the
open-ended question in 4b. FBQs 4c and 4d are open-ended
attitudinal items to find out how the students feel about the various
parts of the guide. These two items deliberately avoid cueing students
towards any particular response. Questions 4e and 4f, like 4c and 4d,

Figure 5.6: FBQ on a List of Prerequisite Terms in a Biology Text

---

FBQ 2

2a   Please explain what you understand by the following terms
(assumed from general knowledge):
    (i)   acceleration
    (ii)   inhibition
    (iii) excitation

2b   If you had difficulty explaining any of the terms in 2a, what did
you do about it?

2c   Without looking back, explain what you understand by the following
terms (introduced in a previous text):
    (i)   haemoglobin
    (ii)   pH
    (iii) habituation

2d   If you had difficulty explaining any of the terms in 2c, what did
you do about it?

ANY OTHER COMMENTS?

---

both seek expressions of opinion without leading the students towards
any specific answer.

FBQ 5 in Figure 5.9 is designed to evaluate a discursive introductory
section of an audiotape, but could readily be adapted for use with any
other introduction (for example, with that of a text). Like FBQ 4 in
Figure 5.8, it includes a series of questions which avoid cueing students'
responses. Questions 5a-5c seek data on clarity; 5c is noteworthy as
one of the few cases where a closed-ended question is useful. Questions
5d-5f, again beginning with a closed-ended filter, gauge students'
feelings about the motivational function of the introduction (attitude
data).

FBQs on the Main Body of Teaching Material

FBQs to evaluate the main body of teaching material must obviously
vary enormously according to the nature and style of the material. For
example, FBQs inserted into a discursive text in a humanities discipline

Figure 5.7: FBQ on a Concept Map in an Education Text

FBQ 3

3a   What do you think the author intended you to do with this
        concept map?

3b   Did you find the map helpful at this stage of your study?

                        Yes   (   )
                        No   (   )

        Please explain your answer.

3c   Which are the starting and finishing points in the diagram?

3d   What do you take to be the significance of the shaded boxes in
        the diagram?

3e   Please list any terms which you do not understand.

ANY OTHER COMMENTS?

Figure 5.8: FBQ on a Study Guide

FBQ 4

4a   Has the Study Guide given you a clear idea about how the text is
        structured?

                        Yes   (   )
                        No   (   )

4b   If not, which parts of the Guide are not clear?

4c   Which parts of the Guide did you like the most?

4d   Which parts did you like the least?

4e   What information, if any, was missing from the Guide which you
        would have liked to be included?

4f   Which parts, if any, of the Guide did you find redundant?

ANY OTHER COMMENTS?

Figure 5.9: FBQ on a Discursive Introduction

FBQ 5

5a   Was the introduction on the audiotape completely clear to you?

Yes   (   )

No   (   )

5b   If there was anything which was not clear, please make a note of it here.

5c   Did you find the speaker's pace:

too fast?   (   )

about right?   (   )

too slow?   (   )

5d   Has the introduction stimulated your interest in the contents of the remainder of the tape?

Yes   (   )

No   (   )

5e   If 'Yes', what did you find particularly stimulating?

5f   If 'No', please say what specifically put you off.

ANY OTHER COMMENTS?

---

will bear little resemblance to those for a highly-structured text in a science, and both will differ greatly from a set of FBQs written to evaluate the main body of a film designed to teach an engineering skill. In this section, therefore, ten examples of FBQs written to evaluate the main body of materials from a wide variety of subject-matter, presented through several different media, will be discussed in order to illustrate the flexibility of the approach.

The first three examples, FBQs 6-8 in Figures 5.10-5.12, relate to teaching material which is expository in style, presented either through the medium of text or of television. FBQ 6 (Figure 5.10) is an example of a question designed to evaluate a section of text in home economics, written for secondary school classes, in which the author is introducing the idea of 'complete' and 'incomplete' proteins. The purpose of the first question (6a) is to determine what students think are the main points (performance). With a section of text that is loosely structured, it is useful to be able to compare what students perceive the main

Figure 5.10: FBQ on a Section of an Expository Home Economics Text

---

FBQ 6

6a   Please summarise briefly what you think are the main points of section 2.

6b   Was section 2 clear to you?

        Yes   (   )

        No   (   )

6c   If not, please say briefly what was not clear.

6d   Do you have any suggestions for how any of these sections might have been made clearer?

6e   Was the number of examples in this section:

        too few?   (   )

        about right?   (   )

        too many?   (   )

6f   Did you find section 2 interesting, boring, or what?

6g   Did you find section 2 too difficult, too easy, just right, or what?

ANY OTHER COMMENTS?

---

points to be with what the author intends them to be. Question 6b acts as a filter to 6c, and is concerned with the clarity of the section. In question 6d, students are given an opportunity to suggest how the teaching might be improved. This type of question is particularly useful. It is surprising how often students suggest creative ways in which materials can be changed which authors eventually adopt in their revisions: Chapter 6 will provide several examples of such student-generated revisions. FBQ 6e asks students to react to the number of examples in the section (attitude), and 6f and 6g are also attitude questions, assessing student feeling towards the section as a whole.

FBQ 7 in Figure 5.11 was written to evaluate 25 pages of uninterrupted text in which six characters carry on an imaginary debate about religious language. The author tells students that, at the end of the debate, they will be asked to summarise the way in which the six disputants would answer the same question. Question 7a is an

Figure 5.11: FBQ on a Section of Text in the Form of a Debate on Religious Language

---

FBQ 7

7a   You'll probably have noticed that for the first time in this text, 25 pages of prose are uninterrupted by any questions or exercises. How do you feel about this?

7b   How many times did you read the debate (or parts of it) before attempting the summary?

Once	( )
Twice	( )
Three times	( )
More than three times	( )

7c   How long (roughly) did you spend on the debate?

( ) minutes

7d   We would like your views on the debate. I have suggested three headings under which you might want to consider it, but please feel free to include any others that occur to you.

(i)   the use of debate as a way of expressing ideas in a text

(ii)   the difficulty or ease with which you understood the ideas

(iii)   the style in which the debate is written

(iv)

(v)

7e   What suggestions do you have on improving the debate as a way of teaching?

ANY OTHER COMMENTS?

---

attitudinal item which attempts to find out how these students, accustomed to a more active mode of learning, react to a long unbroken prose passage. In questions 7b and 7c, the students are asked whether they read the debate more than once (action) and how long they spent on it (time). FBQ 7d asks students to comment on three specific aspects of the debate (attitude again). On this particular question, structuring the students' responses under the three headings is probably a more useful format than an open-ended question simply asking

Figure 5.12: FBQ on a Philosophy Television Programme

FBQ 8

8a   What, in your view, was the *purpose* of the programme?

8b   How successful was the programme in achieving that purpose?

8c   Were you able to understand and follow the arguments:
          In the song? Yes   (   )   In the discussion?   Yes   (   )
                        No   (   )   No   (   )

8d   If anything was not clear, please give details.

8e   This programme was presented in the form of a discussion. How did
          you react to this type of presentation?

8f   What was your overall reaction to the programme?

ANY OTHER COMMENTS?

---

students for their views on the debate, but students are also free to include their own headings. The final question (7e) invites suggestions for improving the debate as a way of teaching.

FBQ 8 in Figure 5.12 is a question designed to evaluate a 25-minute television programme entitled 'Moral responsibility'. The programme was related to printed material introducing philosophy as an area of study in the Arts. It was presented in the form of a discussion between three philosophers. The topic was whether a crime could be said to be a wilful act, or a symptom of a disease. 'Sergeant Krupke's song' from *West Side Story* was used to lead into the topic and students were given the words of the song printed out. The speakers took varied points of view, but it could not be said that any one speaker presented a 'for' or 'against' stance: different individuals introduced particular points into the argument as it progressed. FBQ 8a is a clarity item and 8b is a related attitudinal question. 8c and 8d are the usual type of clarity items and 8e and 8f again seek attitude data.

The next three FBQs relate to textual and audiovisual teaching materials in which students are referred to other parallel materials. For example, FBQ 9 (Figure 5.13) is designed to evaluate a self-instructional text in materials science in which students are required to study

Figure 5.13: FBQ on the Use of a Set Book in Materials Science

---

FBQ 9

9a   This text was structured around a set book and suggested a
       particular strategy for studying the material. Did you follow the
       author's suggested strategy?

                    Yes   (   )
                    No   (   )

9b   If you did, please comment on whether you found it to be an
       effective way of studying a set book.

9c   If you did *not* follow the suggested strategy, please describe the
       particular strategy you did adopt and comment on its effectiveness.

9d   Did you like the idea of studying a set book in this structured way
       or would you have preferred the book to be written as a teaching
       text? Please explain your answer.

9e   Did you find the set book itself to be a stimulating way to
       introduce you to the subject of Materials Science?

                    Yes   (   )
                    No   (   )

       Please explain your answer.

ANY OTHER COMMENTS?

---

selected parts of a set book in parallel with the self-instructional text.
Before each set reading, the author specified those sections he
considered to be essential and indicated those which students could
omit if they were short of time. Each set reading was also preceded
by one or two general questions which were intended to help focus the
students' thoughts as they studied. The following section of text then
provided answers to these questions and summarised other key points
made in the reading. The first question (9a) is a filter to discover whether
students followed the author's suggested learning strategy, the second
(9b) asks those students who did to comment on its effectiveness, and
the third (9c) asks those who pursued a different strategy to describe
it and comment on its effectiveness. These questions seeking action
data are designed to discover what alternative study strategies students
pursued in addition to the one specified by the author. For example,
responses to FBQ 9c indicated that several students preferred to read

the questions, answers and summary before tackling the relevant chapter of the book, making their own list of what they considered to be the most important points and comparing them with the answers and summary afterwards. Other students preferred to read the set book first, then answer the questions and lastly compare their answers with the author's. In revising the materials, the author was able to suggest that students might like to pursue any of three alternative ways of studying the set book in parallel with the self-instructional text. Questions 9d and 9e seek attitude data, assessing students' feelings towards studying a set book in a structured way, and towards this particular set book.

FBQ 10 in Figure 5.14 is an example of a feedback question written to evaluate a section of a classics text in which the author frequently asks the students to refer to parallel teaching material, including parts of two books, some primary source material, and a map. The section deals with the political differences between Sparta and Athens in fifth-century Greece, and the author concludes the section by drawing an analogy between the politics of fifth-century Greece and those of the twentieth century. The first question (10a) is a clarity item, investigating whether students can perceive the overall purpose of the author in the first part of the section. If this question had been presented in a closed-ended format, it might have unnecessarily cued students to the author's purpose. FBQs 10b and 10c are also concerned with clarity. FBQs 10d and 10e assess student reaction to the author's advice to look up references to primary source material (action): *which* references were followed up (10d) and *why* students did not follow up some of the references (10e). Questions 10f and 10g are attitudinal, inviting students to comment on the relevance of the references. In a similar way, questions 10h-10k are designed to discover whether students referred to specified passages in one of the set books and which of these they found to be relevant. FBQs 10l-10n seek action and attitude data on the author's references to a map. Question 10p invited students to express their feelings about the concluding analogy (attitude). The final two questions (10q and 10r) are aimed at finding out what students intend to do about the author's instruction to read three chapters in the second set book (action). These questions are important because the author assumes, in the next section of text, that all students will have read these chapters as instructed.

FBQ 11 (Figure 5.15) is intended to evaluate a short radiovision sequence in earth science, dealing with the use of aerial photography. Students were provided with a package containing stereo-pairs of photographs, transparent overlays and a simple stereoscope. They were

Figure 5.14: FBQ on the Use of Parallel Teaching Materials in a Classics Text

---

FBQ 10

10a   Can you briefly state the purpose of the first part of the text (pp.1-6)?

10b   Were pp.1-6 completely clear to you?

        Yes   (   )

        No   (   )

10c   If not, please say exactly what was unclear.

10d   Did you follow up the author's references to the primary source material?

        All   (   )

        Some (   )   Which?. . . . .

        None (   )

10e   If you didn't follow up all of them, why not?

10f   Did you find all the references you looked up relevant in the context in which they were mentioned?

        Yes   (   )

        No   (   )

10g   If not, which ones did you find irrelevant and why?

10h   Did you follow the author's advice to read the extracts mentioned in the text from Thucydides' *The Peloponnesian War?*

        All   (   )

        Some (   )   Which?. . . . .

        None (   )

10i   If you didn't follow up all of them, why not?

10j   Did you find all the extracts you read relevant in the context in which they were mentioned?

        Yes   (   )

        No   (   )

10k   If not, which did you find irrelevant and why?

10l   Did you consult Map 7?

        Once   (   )

        Twice   (   )

        Not at all   (   )

Figure 5.14 *(contd.)*

10m Did you find the Map helpful?

Yes ( )

No ( )

10n What problems, if any, did you have with it?

10p How do you feel about the author's analogy between Greek history and our own experience of international politics?

10q Have you read Chapters 9-11 of Burn's *History of Greece?*

Yes ( )

No ( )

10r If not, do you intend to do so?

Yes, before reading further ( )

Yes, at some later point ( )

No ( )

ANY OTHER COMMENTS?

Figure 5.15: FBQ on a Radiovision Programme in Earth Science

FBQ 11

11a Did you complete the preparatory materials before the programme?

Yes ( )

No ( )

11b How useful was this material in helping you to understand the content of the programme?

11c When using the stereoscope while listening to the programme, were you satisfied that you were:

Able to see stereovision?

yes, always ( )

most of the time ( )

some of the time only ( )

no, never ( )

don't know ( )

Figure 5.15 *(contd.)*

11c *(contd.)*	*Able to locate all the features mentioned?*	
	yes, all of them	( )
	most of them	( )
	a few of them only	( )
	none of them	( )
	don't know	( )

11d   When using the stereoscope, did you have any problems with concentration?

Yes   (   )

No   (   )

If 'yes', please explain

11e   The programme worked through *five* stereo-pairs of aerial photographs, using the stereoscope.

Did you find the time given to locate each feature was:

too little   (   )

about right   (   )

too much   (   )

don't know   (   )

11f   Please refer to FRAME 3, REEL 2, of your aerial photographs. Place the photographs in the stereoscope and turn to FRAME 3. Using the stereoscope, please DRAW on the grid the following features from FRAME 3.

(i)   The path

(ii)   The boundary between the dark rock and the pale rock at the top left-hand part of the picture.

(iii)   The linear features running up to the boundary.

(iv)   The location of X.

11g   What are your feelings about radiovision as a means for studying Earth Science material?

ANY OTHER COMMENTS?

expected to have read some preparatory materials and completed some exercises involving the use of the stereoscope before studying the radiovision sequence. The purpose of the latter was to teach students the method of isolating topographical and geological features through the examination of aerial photographs. By means of the radio broadcast, students were instructed to look through the stereoscope and, with comments from the presenter, to locate certain features on five pairs of photographs. The procedure was for the presenter to talk students through the observations, pointing out relevant features, and allowing some time for them to be located.

FBQ 11a asks students what they did about the preparatory material (action), and FBQ 11b asks whether they found it to be useful (attitude). Question 11c asks students about the operation of the stereoscope (action), and 11d whether they had any problems with concentration. FBQ 11e is on the pacing of the radio programme (time) and 11f is a performance question to determine whether students had actually been able to locate some of the features referred to. The final question (11g) is concerned with student reaction to radiovision as a means for studying Earth Science material.

The next four FBQs illustrate different ways of evaluating learning materials which encourage students to become more actively involved in the learning process. The first of these (Figures 5.16 and 5.17) is concerned with a design task in which each student was asked to draw a scale plan of his own house. A time estimate of two hours was suggested for the task. Squared paper was provided and the author offered a number of suggestions on how to proceed (e.g. begin with one room and record its overall measurements including features such as windows and doors; repeat this process for every other room; complete the plan by plotting the relationships and spaces between rooms). With such an open-ended activity, an author of a self-instructional text could obviously give little feedback to students on how successful they had been. He did, however, provide a scale plan of his own house as a model with which they could compare their efforts. The FBQ is in two parts following the pattern outlined in Figure 5.4 (p.104): FBQ 12.1 (Figure 5.16) to be completed after the students have finished the task and FBQ 12.2 (Figure 5.17) to be completed after they have compared their efforts with the author's model. FBQ 12.1a simply asks the students to submit their completed plans — a performance question which enables the evaluator to analyse the students' efforts and discover how successful they were with the task. In so far as they were unsuccessful, he can then determine where they

Figure 5.16: FBQ on a Design Activity

FBQ 12.1

12.1a Please attach your scale plan to this FBQ.

12.1b Approximately how long did you spend on this activity?

(   )   hours

12.1c Were the author's directions clear?

Yes (   )

No   (   )

12.1d If not, please say what was unclear.

ANY OTHER COMMENTS?

Figure 5.17: FBQ on Model Answer to a Design Activity

FBQ 12.2

12.2a What use did you make of the author's model answer
(i.e. his scale plan)?

12.2b What was your overall reaction to this activity?

ANY OTHER COMMENTS?

---

may have gone astray. Question 12.1b seeks data on time, and
questions 12.1c and 12.1d concern the clarity of the author's
instructions. In the second part of the FBQ (Figure 5.17), students are
asked an action question about how they used the author's model
answer (12.2a) and an attitude question about their reaction to the
activity as a whole (12.2b).

FBQ 13 (Figure 5.18) is designed to evaluate student response to
two different teaching techniques used within the same section of a
self-instructional philosophy text: both are designed to encourage
students to be actively involved in learning the material. The first part
of this section included four questions which the student was asked to

Figure 5.18: FBQ on a Philosophy Text Including Questions to the Student

---

FBQ 13

13a   Were the following subsections clear to you?

4.1	Murder	Yes ( )	No ( )
4.2	Criminal unpunished	Yes ( )	No ( )
4.3	Innocent punished	Yes ( )	No ( )
4.4	The examiner's case	Yes ( )	No ( )
4.5	Promise-keeping	Yes ( )	No ( )
4.6	Anti-social acts	Yes ( )	No ( )

13b   If any of them were not clear, please say briefly exactly what was not clear.

13c   Can you suggest any ways in which the material might be improved?

13d   In sections 4.1 (Murder) and 4.2 (Criminal unpunished) the author asked you to answer four questions before reading on. Did you try to answer these for yourself?

Question 1   Yes ( )   No ( )
Question 2   Yes ( )   No ( )
Question 3   Yes ( )   No ( )
Question 4   Yes ( )   No ( )

13e   If you did not try any of them, please say briefly why not.

13f   If you did try to answer some of them in what way, if at all, did you find this helpful?

13g   In sections 4.5 and 4.6, did you follow the dialogues as suggested by the author, uncovering them line by line and trying to answer the author's questions before reading on?

Section 4.5   Yes ( )   No ( )
Section 4.6   Yes ( )   No ( )

13h   If you did not try any of them, please say briefly why not.

13i   If you did try to answer some of them in what way, if at all, did you find this helpful?

13j   Which of the two styles of writing do you prefer and why?
Occasional questions   ( )
Dialogue with questions   ( )
Didn't like either   ( )

ANY OTHER COMMENTS?

---

answer for himself before reading on. The second part consisted of a 'Socratic dialogue' in which several steps in the dialogue were omitted and the student was invited to fill in the missing steps. The section of text, entitled 'The problems for utilitarianism', included six short subsections, and the first two questions (13a and 13b) are therefore a variant on the FBQ pattern of asking students whether one particular section was clear. FBQ 13c is the usual type inviting suggestions for improvement. Questions 13d-13f are to evaluate students' action and attitude in response to the first teaching technique, whilst questions 13g-13i gauge reaction to the second technique. The final attitudinal question (13j) asks students to express their preference between the two techniques.

FBQ 14 in Figure 5.19 is an example of a feedback question written to evaluate a 50-minute television programme entitled 'Patterns of inequality: A woman's work'. The programme exemplified ways in which sexual inequality has become institutionalised in society, in order to explore the underlying ideology. The primary emphasis was on women's work outside the home as part-time or full-time employees. Two particular industrial settings were considered in detail: a manufacturing industry and the television industry. To help students retain important points from the television material, the author of the programme suggested that the students follow various activities before, during and after the programme. Before viewing, students were asked to read some related textual material. During the programme, the author suggested that they take notes on some of the basic questions raised and the kinds of explanations offered by people with opinions on sexual inequality. After the programme, students were asked (i) to transcribe their list of questions and explanations onto a form provided by the author, (ii) to read an article related to the programme, (iii) to redraft their list in the light of the article and their pre-television reading, (iv) to compare their list with the author, and (v) to answer six questions about sexual inequality.

FBQs 14a-14d are attitudinal items which ask for the students' opinions on the particular teaching approach adopted in the programme. Questions 14e-14k all seek action data about the various activities suggested to students by the author. The questions are designed to find out whether students did pursue the activities and, if they did not, what their reasons were. FBQ 14l asks students' opinions of the value of the activities (attitude).

FBQ 15 (Figure 5.20) deals with a section of text written around Charlotte Bronte's novel *Jane Eyre*, in which the author tries to engage

Figure 5.19: FBQ on a Television Programme in Sociology

FBQ 14

14a   The programme did not set out to teach directly but presented a range of material about inequality. How did you react to this approach?

14b   Do you think that the inclusion of two case studies (based on the manufacturing and broadcasting industries) was worthwhile or not?

        Yes   (   )

        No   (   )

Please explain the reasons for your answer.

14c   Do you think that the length of the programme was appropriate?

        Yes   (   )

        No   (   )

Please explain the reasons for your answer.

14d   Do you think that the programme reflected an overall ideology with regard to sexual inequality?

        Yes   (   )

        No   (   )

   Don't know (   )

Please explain your answer.

14e   *Before* viewing, did you follow the author's suggestion to read the associated printed material?

        Yes   (   )

        No   (   )

If not, why not?

14f   *During* the programme, did you note down questions raised and/or explanations given?

Took notes throughout   (   )

Started to take notes, but stopped (   ) Why? _____

Intended to take notes, but didn't (   )   _____

Didn't try to take notes   (   )   _____

Figure 5.19 *(contd.)*

14g   *After* the programme, did you write up your notes of the questions and explanations on the sheet provided by the author?

Yes   (   )

No   (   )   Why? _____

Didn't have notes   (   )   _____

_____

14h   Did you read the article by Stuart Hall after watching the programme?

Yes   (   )

No, but intend to   (   )

Don't intend to   (   )

14i   If 'yes', what if anything did you do about the suggestion to redraft what you had written in the light of your reading of this article?

14j   Did you compare your own list of questions and explanations with the author's?

Yes   (   )

No, but intend to   (   )   _____

Don't intend to   (   ) Why? _____

Didn't make a list of my own (   )   _____

14k   Did you attempt any of the six questions suggested by the author? (Please tick ONE box in EACH row.)

Study Question	Yes	No, but intend to	Don't intend to
1	( )	( )	( )
2	( )	( )	( )
3	( )	( )	( )
4	( )	( )	( )
5	( )	( )	( )
6	( )	( )	( )

14l   Which of the activities associated with the programme did you find (a) particularly helpful and (b) a relative waste of time in relation to your study of inequality.

(a)   particularly helpful

(b)   a relative waste of time

ANY OTHER COMMENTS?

Figure 5.20: FBQ on a Literature Text including Learning Activities

---

FBQ 15

15a   On page 33 the author asked you to list all the places in the novel which are about education. Did you do so?

         Yes   (   )

         No   (   )

15b   If you did, roughly how long did this take you?

         (   )   minutes

15c   If you didn't, why not?

15d   Was the material in subsections 2.1 and 2.2 clear to you?

     2.1   Yes   (   )   2.2   Yes   (   )

         No   (   )   No   (   )

15e   If not, please indicate what was not clear to you.

     2.1

     2.2

15f   On pages 40-43, the author raised five questions for your consideration. To answer them, she suggested that you search through the novel for 'evidence'. How did you react to this activity? (e.g. Did you search through the novel and then write your answers to the questions? Did you think about the questions without referring back to the novel? Did you read on ignoring the questions?)

15g   On page 45, the author asked you to write a detailed plan for an essay on 'The theme of education in *Jane Eyre*'. Did you do so?

         Yes   (   )

         No   (   )

15h   If you did, roughly how long did this take you?

         (   )   minutes

15i   If not, please say why not.

15j   How do you feel about this exercise?

15k   Look back over this section. Are there any points, or arguments, the author makes that you strongly disagree with?

         Yes   (   )

         No   (   )

15l   If 'yes', please specify and comment.

ANY OTHER COMMENTS?

---

students in various activities as they work through the teaching material. Questions 15a, 15f and 15g are to determine whether students did, in fact, become actively involved (action), questions 15b and 15h to estimate how long the activities took (time), and questions 15c, 15i and 15j to examine how students felt about them (attitude). FBQs 15d and 15e are clarity questions designed to determine whether students had any problems with two subsections which the author thought might present special difficulties. The final two questions (15k and 15l) were asked because the author wanted to know whether most of the students agreed with the points she was making.

FBQs on Retrospective Organisers

Figures 5.21-5.23 are examples of FBQs to evaluate three types of retrospective organisers: a summary, a checklist of technical terms and their definitions, and a self-assessment post-test. FBQ 16 (Figure 5.21) on the summary is straightforward. Questions 16a and 16b ask students to comment on the clarity of the summary, while 16c and 16d ask whether the summary is sufficiently complete. In the last question (16e), students are asked whether they feel the summary has been a helpful learning aid.

In FBQ 17, to evaluate a checklist of technical terms, students are asked to describe how they actually used the list (17a) and how much time they spent on it (17b). In the next question (17c), they are asked to compare their own personal list of difficult technical terms with the terms in the checklist. The author can use responses to this FBQ to compile the final version of the checklist. The last question (17d) elicits the students' subjective feelings about the helpfulness of the checklist.

FBQ 18 is on a self-assessment post-test. The first set of questions (18a-18c) ask students to describe what they did with the post-test (action). In the second set, students are asked to comment on the clarity of the questions (18d-18e) and on the clarity of the author's specimen answers (18f-18g). FBQs 18h and 18i are performance questions to find out where and how students' answers differed from the author's. Responses to 18i may enable the author, when revising the post-test, both to anticipate alternative correct answers and to provide a discussion of the most common incorrect answers. FBQ 18j is another action question designed to find out what students did if their answers did not conform to the author's (e.g. Did they re-read the relevant parts of the text, try to find other related material, or contact their tutor?). The final item (18k) seeks attitude data on the usefulness of the post-test.

Figure 5.21: FBQ on a Summary

FBQ 16

16a Has the summary given you a clear idea of the main points covered in this chapter?

Yes (   )

No (   )

16b If not, which parts of the summary were not clear?

16c In your opinion, has the summary adequately covered all the main points discussed in the chapter?

Yes (   )

No (   )

16d If not, what further points do you think should be added to the summary?

16e Do you feel that the summary has been a helpful aid to learning?

Yes (   )

No (   )

Please explain your answer.

ANY OTHER COMMENTS?

Figure 5.22: FBQ on a Checklist

FBQ 17

17a What use did you make of the checklist of technical terms? (Did you ignore the list, read through the complete list of terms and definitions, skim through the terms but ignore the definitions, or what?)

17b Approximately how long did you spend on the checklist?

(   )   minutes

17c At the beginning of the text, you were asked to list any terms discussed in the text which you didn't understand. If there are any terms on your list which are *not* included in the checklist, please list them here.

17d Has the checklist been a helpful aid to learning? Please explain your answer.

ANY OTHER COMMENTS?

Figure 5.23: FBQ on a Self-assessment Post-test

FBQ 18

18a   Did you try to answer *all* ten of the questions in the self-assessment post-test?

Yes   (   )

No   (   )

18b   If not, please say which ones you did not try to answer and why?

18c   For those questions you did attempt, did you answer them in writing, think about an answer, or what?

18d   Were all of the questions in the post-test clear (i.e. did you understand what each question was asking you to do)?

Yes   (   )

No   (   )

18e   If not, which questions were not clear?

18f   Were all of the author's answers to the post-test questions clear?

Yes   (   )

No   (   )

18g   If not, which answers were not clear?

18h   Which of your answers agreed with the author's?

1   (   )   6   (   )

2   (   )   7   (   )

3   (   )   8   (   )

4   (   )   9   (   )

5   (   )   10   (   )

18i   Please write those of your answers which differed from the author's here.

18j   What did you do if you got any answers wrong?

18k   Has the post-test helped you to assess your own understanding of the material covered in the text?

Yes   (   )

No   (   )

Please explain your answer.

ANY OTHER COMMENTS?

The Presentation of FBQs to Students

As indicated in Chapter 3, in-text feedback questions are valuable as a means of collecting data in student try-out because they require students to react to a relatively small segment of teaching material while the experience of it is still fresh in their minds. Having decided what evaluative data are required on a particular piece of teaching material and where the FBQs should be located to collect these data, the question arises of how the FBQs should be physically presented to the try-out students.

In the case of printed teaching materials the authors have used two methods of presenting the FBQs. The first of these is to interleave FBQs into the text itself, preferably distinguishing them from the teaching material itself by printing them on different-coloured paper and numbering them as 'A' pages. Thus the text studied by try-out students consists of a few pages of teaching material (say, pp.1-4), a coloured page with an FBQ (p.4A), a few more pages of teaching material (say, pp.5-10), a coloured page with another FBQ (p.10A), and so on. Using separate coloured pages for FBQs has two advantages: first, students can easily identify them, and secondly, they can be readily removed by students for return to the evaluator, leaving students with a complete text for future reference.

While interleaving FBQs in the text is a perfectly satisfactory way of presenting them to students, there are occasions when it is not feasible for operational reasons (for example, it may require re-typing or extensive cutting and pasting of the draft). A second method is to mark the text at each point where an FBQ is to be answered, directing students to turn to the appropriate FBQ in a separately bound booklet. For example, coloured stickers reading 'PLEASE DO FBQ X NOW' can be attached to the text at the relevant points: it is obviously important that such directions are eye-catching. This method is slightly more tedious for the student, because he has to move backwards and forwards between the text and a separate booklet of FBQs, but this has not been found to be a serious problem (Nathenson, 1979).

The methods for presenting FBQs on audiovisual materials vary according to the length and nature of the materials. If the tape, film, television programme, etc. is of relatively short duration (say, up to about 30 minutes), it may be that the evaluator does not wish to seek any feedback until the end of the teaching sequence. In this case, the set of FBQs can be presented to try-out students in the form of a printed questionnaire to be completed immediately after students have finished studying the materials.

The evaluator may, however, feel that it is important to collect feedback at intermediate points during an audiovisual teaching sequence. This will normally be the case if the study time is expected to be longer than about 30 minutes, and may be so even with shorter sequences if immediacy of response is critical. The FBQs must then be interpolated in the audiovisual materials much as they normally are in textual materials. Two methods of presentation are possible. The FBQ can be presented in the medium of the teaching material, e.g. read by the presenter on an audiotape or on the sound-track of a film or videotape, or presented as a visual on a slide or on the television or film screen. Alternatively, the audiotape, film, or videotape can include an aural or visual cue to stop the tape or film and answer the relevant FBQ in a separate printed document. The latter is a more convenient method of presentation in most cases.

In Summary

This chapter has introduced a set of procedures for preparing in-text feedback questions and has offered examples of FBQs used to evaluate learning materials presented through various media and concerned with a variety of subject-matters. Its key points can be summarised in the form of the following 'rules-of-thumb'.

1. Analyse the learning materials into:

Preliminary organisers	• objectives
	• list of new and/or prerequisite terms
	• concept map
	• study guide
	• introduction
Main body	• sections and/or subsections of the learning material
Retrospective organisers	• summary
	• checklist of terms
	• self-assessment post-test.

2. In consultation with the author:
   (a)   Identify the intended teaching function of each of these;
   (b)   Predict as wide a range as possible of the problems students may encounter in studying, in terms of performance, clarity, level, action, attitude and time; and
   (c)   Select those potential problems which are likely to be most critical for formulation as FBQs.

3. Decide on the location of FBQs within the learning materials. This
   will normally be:

For preliminary organisers	— immediately after the preliminary organiser and at the end of the materials;
For the main body	— at the end of the author's sections or subsections, but sufficiently often to enable students to react to the section while it is fresh in their minds;
For retrospective organisers	— immediately after the retrospective organiser.

4. Formulate FBQs so that the responses are likely to provide data
   which will be useful in undertaking revision.
5. Use open-ended questions except:
   (a) When the processing of responses will be simplified by the use
       of filter questions; or
   (b) When it is known that there can only be a limited range of
       possible responses.
6. Provide cues or prompts only when necessary to clarify the question
   or when it is desirable to focus students' responses.
7. Whenever possible, cast FBQs in performance terms rather than
   seeking students' opinions of how well they have understood the
   materials.
8. Seek students' suggestions for improvement.
9. Include an 'Any other comments?' item in every FBQ.
10. Present FBQs in such a way that students are encouraged to answer
    them immediately.

Whilst these rules-of-thumb and their elaboration in this chapter may
be useful guides to the preparation of in-text feedback questions,
writing effective FBQs can only be learnt through practice. In training
other evaluators in this skill, the authors have found the following
procedures valuable. First, at least two (and preferably more) evaluators
independently prepare a set of FBQs on the same segment of learning
materials. Then they get together to compare their efforts, discussing
their positioning of the FBQs within the materials, their reasons for
selecting particular issues to explore in the questions, and their choices
of question format and wording. After two or three iterations on
different kinds of learning materials, a reasonable degree of consistency
begins to be achieved. Practitioners reading this book will find this a
useful approach to acquiring the skill of writing FBQs prior to the next
step in student try-out: analysing students' responses and transforming

them into revisions.

Notes

1. The authors are indebted to the Open University for permission to reprint this Figure, which appeared in Block 1, 'Language variation and English', of Course E262 *Language and Learning.*

2. In the form in which this, and subsequent examples of FBQs are presented to try-out students, appropriate spaces are left between each FBQ for students to write their answers.

6 TRANSFORMING FEEDBACK DATA INTO REVISIONS

The final stage of student try-out involves analysing the data (from in-text and post-text feedback questions, assessment material, interviews, etc.) and making revision decisions based on this analysis. This sometimes presents little difficulty. For example, if the majority of students write, in response to an FBQ inviting suggestions for improvement, that they believe they would have been helped by a worked example, the revision required is clear and can be easily carried out. Or again, if a substantial proportion of try-out students offer free comments to the effect that a particular section of a text or film added nothing to their understanding, the evaluator will recommend to the author that this section be deleted. Such clear indications for revision do often emerge when using the integrated feedback system.

However, data analysis is not always so straightforward. Responses to open-ended FBQs may reflect a wide range of problems encountered by the students, perhaps with contradictory suggestions or implications for revision. Content analysis of such open-ended data to identify the crucial points made by students is time-consuming and requires considerable skill. Nor, once the data have been analysed, do they always point clearly to one particular revision which will overcome the difficulty. Just as subjective decisions have to be made when deciding which issues to explore in try-out, so analysis of feedback data and decisions about revision will involve a substantial subjective element — an evaluation of the evaluative data, which Kandaswamy (undated) describes as 'meta-evaluation'.

The relationship between the evaluator and author (if the roles are separated) is perhaps at its most critical at this stage of try-out. In some cases the evaluator may go as far as making recommendations for revision based on his analysis of the data. In others it may be impossible or inappropriate for the evaluator to go further than presenting his analysis of the data, leaving the author to make his own judgements as to the revisions which should be undertaken, or even whether or not revision is necessary. In any event, evaluator and author have to work closely together.

Revision of learning materials, no less than their origination, remains an essentially creative process. The authors have not found attempts to provide detailed prescriptions for revision (e.g. Gropper, 1975) very helpful. This chapter, therefore, does not attempt to be prescriptive about the revision process. However, the authors have found it helpful to systematise the analysis of feedback data and the search for appropriate revisions to some extent by first examining outcome data (i.e. performance), and then by considering sequentially the different types of process data (i.e. clarity, level, action, attitude and time). In the first part of this chapter, a simple algorithmic representation of this systematisation is described. In the remainder of the chapter, the process of transforming feedback data into revisions is illustrated by six substantial examples. Each of these presents the raw data arising from one of the sample FBQs given in Chapter 5, describes how the evaluator analysed it, and presents the recommendations for revision that emerged from his analysis.

A Data-processing Algorithm

The simple algorithm in Figure 6.1 illustrates a partially systematic procedure for analysing the potentially large amount of data generated by the integrated feedback system. It combines an examination of student performance measures with an analysis of the data collected via in-text FBQs, and has proved a useful aid both in identifying problems in learning materials and in seeking solutions to such problems. The first step is to determine whether performance data are available relating to the particular segment of learning materials under consideration — for example, in the form of results of summative assessment, post-test FBQs or in-text self-assessment items. If such data are available, the next step is to determine by analysis of these performance data whether an acceptable proportion of the try-out students have successfully met the performance criterion specified by the author of the materials.

If no performance data are available (route III in Figure 6.1), or performance data are available which indicates that the author's criterion has not been met (route II), each part of the related FBQ(s) is examined. In general, it is useful to examine first those parts of the FBQs which seek data on clarity, then data on level, action, attitude and time in that order. Even if performance data are available which indicate that the required criterion has been met (route I), it is still necessary to examine the various parts of related in-text FBQs to see if any revisions are indicated to improve the quality of the learning experience for students. The fact that students reach the performance criterion is not enough; they may, for example, have found the material

Figure 6.1: A Data-processing Algorithm

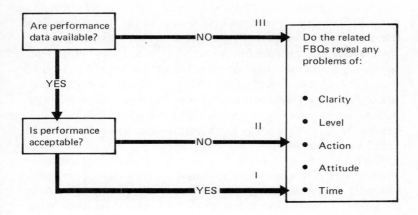

too easy (level), or boring (attitude), or it may have taken them too long (time).

Three brief examples of the processing of data from the try-out of an Open University introductory music course will demonstrate the three alternative routes through the algorithm. The first of these illustrates route I, and shows why it is important to examine FBQs even when performance data are satisfactory. One of the objectives of the course was to teach students to name notes on treble and bass staves. The related teaching material involved students in memorising four mnemonics associated with the lines and spaces of the two staves (e.g. *E*very *G*ood *B*oy *D*eserves *F*ood for the five lines of the treble stave). Student performance on the related post-test item revealed that 95 per cent of students could successfully meet the objective of naming notes on both staves. The related FBQ included clarity, level and action questions. Examination of the responses suggested that the teaching text was clear and that most students considered the level appropriate. But responses to the FBQ item which asked students to describe *how* they had set about learning to name notes on staves (action) indicated that only about half of them had followed the suggested teaching strategy of memorising the mnemonics. The other half had developed their own system of learning, often after spending a considerable time attempting, but failing to commit the mnemonics to memory. Most of these students said that they had mastered the names of the notes by remembering that the bottom line on the treble stave is G (and on the bass stave F) and then counting up and down the lines and spaces alphabetically. What is important about this example is that if the evaluator had looked only at the performance measure and not at *all* of the FBQ items, he would not have discovered the alternate mode of learning and no revisions to the material would have been suggested. The evaluator recommended to the author that both ways of learning how to name notes should be presented as alternatives and that students should be encouraged to select the way they find most convenient. Although it was unlikely that this revision would have much effect on student performance, it could have at least two other benefits: influencing the study strategy that students adopt and reducing study time for a substantial proportion of students.

When performance data are available which indicate that less than an acceptable proportion of the students have reached the criterion (route II), the evaluator turns to the related FBQs to try to determine the source of the problem and to search for a possible solution. In the try-out of the same music course, a post-test item revealed that only about 20 per cent of students had achieved the author's objective of naming the degrees of the musical scale (tonic, supertonic, mediant, etc.). The related FBQ indicated that the relevant section of the teaching text had been quite clear, but there were a large number of comments on an attitudinal item reflecting dissatisfaction with the amount of memorisation which had been required throughout the section. Responses to the 'Any other comments?' item revealed the source of their dissatisfaction. In successive sections of the text, they had been instructed to learn the Italian-English equivalents of a series of musical terms, then to learn the major key signatures, then the minor key signatures, and finally this objective was introduced — to learn the names of the degrees of the scale. It was clear they were losing interest in the material as a result of the heavy load of memorisation required of them. Discussion between the author and evaluator revealed that only two of these memorisation tasks were absolutely essential at this particular point in the course: learning the major key signatures and learning the names of the degrees of the scale. Consequently, it was decided to retain both of these tasks. One task was judged not to be essential at all and was made optional, while another was worked into a later point in the course.

Route III through the algorithm applies when a section of learning material has not been tested by any performance item. In such cases, the evaluator focuses on the FBQs alone, looking sequentially at problems related to clarity, level, action, attitude and time. For example, in one part of the music course, the author introduced the concept of 'phrasing' and the related subconcepts of 'phrases', 'slurs', and 'staccato'. Examination of a related FBQ seeking clarity data indicated that students did not understand the author's distinction between the major phrases of a tune and the detailed phrasing within the phrases. Free comments by two students suggested a clearer way of presenting these concepts.

These brief examples illustrate the systematic analysis of student feedback using the data-processing algorithm and a few of the different types of revision which may result. They also point to a possible way of classifying revisions:

> *Add* an optional learning route (to teach naming of notes on staves);
> *Delete* an objective (not requiring students to undertake one of the memorisation tasks);
> *Move* a section of teaching to another point in the text (one of the memorisation tasks);
> *Modify* an explanation (clarifying the presentation of the concept of 'phrasing').

The authors have found it useful to think of revision in terms of these four categories — add, delete, move or modify.

In the remainder of this chapter, six more elaborate case studies of data analysis and revision are presented. Each is based on one of the FBQs used as examples in Chapter 5: one on a preliminary organiser, four on sections of the main body of different types of learning materials, and one on a retrospective organiser. The responses of a group of try-out students are analysed and revisions suggested. At the end of the chapter, these revisions are described in terms of the above categorisation.

Case Study 1: A List of Objectives

The FBQ in Figure 5.5 (p. 107) can be used to illustrate revisions to what is probably the most common preliminary organiser — a list of objectives. The material being tried out was an introductory text on chemistry, and FBQ 1 was written to evaluate a list of 15 behaviourally-stated objectives placed at the beginning of the text. Since no performance data were available at this early stage of students' study of the materials, route III through the algorithm in Figure 6.1 applied. The evaluator proceeded directly to analysis of data on clarity (FBQ 1d and 1e), action (FBQ 1a), attitude (FBQ 1c and 1f), and time (FBQ 1b), and finally conducted a content analysis of the responses under 'Any other comments?'.

Of the 20 try-out students, 19 indicated that they had some difficulty understanding what was meant by the objectives (i.e. 19 replied 'yes' to the clarity filter question 1d, and only one replied 'no'). These 19 all listed, in FBQ 1e, the specific objective(s) which had presented problems, in most cases with a word or two indicating the nature of the difficulty. The responses to FBQ 1e are summarised in Figure 6.2. Evidently, there were considerable clarity problems.

In FBQ 1a (action) most students identified with one or more of the prompts in the question. Thus 16 students said they had read the objectives rather quickly, two that they had read them more than once, and three that they had read each one carefully (but none that they had made a précis). In addition, seven students went outside the prompts by saying that they planned to re-read the objectives at some point in the future.

Feedback on the attitude item 1c, dealing with students' feelings towards the objectives, illuminated the responses to the action item 1a. Only one student reacted positively: 'I found these objectives useful

Figure 6.2: Summary of Responses to FBQ 1e

Objective	Number of students expressing difficulty	
1	13	Terminology unfamiliar
2	3	Example unclear
3	8	Concept unfamiliar
4	9	Objective unfamiliar
5	19	Terminology unfamiliar
6	6	Concept unfamiliar
7	9	Terminology unfamiliar
8	7	Concept unfamiliar
9	18	Mathematical symbol confusing
10	14	Objective not clearly stated
11	19	Terminology and mathematical symbol unfamiliar
12	10	Example unclear
13	4	Concept unclear
14	12	Terminology unfamiliar
15	13	Objective not stated clearly

because they gave me some indication of what I was going to learn and what I was expected to do.' Ten students took up the cue in FBQ 1c and said they had been 'put off' by the objectives. A further six made a similar point in different words, for example:

> My feeling towards objectives depends on how realistic and relevant the objectives appear to be. The objectives for this text have filled me with apprehension; they make me think that the text will be extremely difficult. I am very worried that I won't be able to achieve all fifteen within the study period.

This generally negative reaction in FBQ 1c was reiterated in 1f, in which 17 students responded negatively to the closed-ended item, indicating that they had not found the objectives helpful as a preliminary organiser. Those who explained their answers reiterated points made in response to other items within the FBQ such as concern about the large number of unfamiliar terms, concepts and symbols involved and their intention to return to the objectives after studying the text.

The data from FBQ 1b (time) indicated that 17 of the 20 students spent ten minutes or less reading the 15 detailed objectives. This again confirmed the majority response to 1a — that most students had given the objectives only cursory attention.

Thus the data from items 1a-1f strongly suggested that this list of objectives had failed in its teaching function as a preliminary organiser, but so far little positive indication of what revision might be undertaken had been provided. The evaluator therefore turned to the responses made in the 'Any other comments?' section of the FBQ. Fifteen of the twenty students had made comments, which are reproduced in full in Figure 6.3.

In order to process these comments, the evaluator followed a three-stage content analysis procedure. First, each comment was subdivided into separate points. In comment A, for example, the evaluator identified three points (as italicised in Figure 6.3). This student finds objectives appearing at the beginning of a text of little use because he does not understand them; he would like to return to the objectives as he works through the text; but in practice he rarely does so. Similarly, comment B contains four separate points, comment C two points, and so on. The second step for the evaluator was to group together those points which seemed to be similar. The three points made in comment A are numbered 1, 2 and 3. In comment B, the first point about finding the objectives alarming is a new point (4); the second, about inserting objectives at relevant points throughout the text, is similar to the second point in comment A and is therefore also numbered 2; the third is another new point (5), suggesting that objectives should be placed at the end of the text; and the fourth, about not in practice returning to the objectives, is numbered 3 because it is similar to the third point in comment A. In the present example, the evaluator considered that all the points made in the 15 comments fell into one of six categories. The third and final step for the evaluator was to summarise the categorised comments as shown in Figure 6.4.

These data from the students' free comments provided the evaluator with very clear pointers to possible revisions to overcome the problems identified by items 1a-1f. In writing his report to the author, the evaluator first summarised the data above and then presented his conclusions from them. His suggestions for revision were as follows:

It is clear, from the responses to items 1a-1f of FBQ 1, that students did not understand the meaning of many of the objectives because they were formulated using unfamiliar terms and concepts. As a result, students gave only cursory attention to the objectives, spent little time on them, and did not find them helpful as a preliminary organiser. In addition, a considerable number of free comments mentioned the incomprehensibility of the objectives and several included negative feelings. However, several students also commented that, in general, they do find a statement of objectives useful at the beginning of a text, though not in the form used here. A majority of students find a formal statement of objectives most useful for reference while studying and as a summary or checklist at the end of the text. They tend, however, to forget to use an initial list of objectives retrospectively in these ways.

Suggestions: (a) Reposition the objectives, in their present form, within the text at the end of each section they relate to (i.e. objectives 1-2 after section 1, objectives 3-5 after section 2, etc.);

(b) Repeat the full list of objectives at the end of the text, so that students can use them as a checklist for revision;

(c) Most of the problems revealed by item 1e about the wording of the objectives should disappear, or at least become much less critical, with the objectives resituated as suggested above — however, the comments in Figure 6.2 suggest that in three cases (objectives 2, 10 and 15) the wording will still be in need of clarification;

(d) Delete the present formal statement of objectives from the

Figure 6.3: Free Comments on FBQ 1

A   They are *of little or no use to me at the start of the text, as invariably
    they mean nothing and I do not understand them.* I look at them in case   (1)
    I may understand them and do in fact *usually intend to return to them
    as I go through the text.* This, however, is *rarely done mainly due to time*   (2)
    constraints and I invariably forget.   (3)

B   I believe objectives are necessary but the number of objectives becomes
    rather alarming at times. I would prefer objectives to be *inserted in*   (4)
    relevant sections throughout the text *and summarised at the end of the*   (2)
    text in a list — 'you should now be able to. . .'. If one cannot, one must   (5)
    look back and find out what is wrong. *But I never return to the objectives*   (3)
    list as a whole to see whether I can.

C   *Objectives are extremely useful* provided they are clearly understood   (6)
    by all students and can be used as a stimulus to further reading. All too
    often the objectives become difficult to read as objectives because of the
    complexity of the phraseology used. Surely objectives should be clear,
    concise, easy to read, simple to understand and directly expressed in lay
    terms. *The objectives in this text are concise but rarely easy to understand.* (1)

D   Before studying the text, a lot of *the terms used in the statements of
    objectives are unfamiliar to me.* Therefore I read through them quickly   (1)
    and refer back to them whilst studying the text.   (2)

E   Objectives *give me some idea of how tough a text will be,* but! after the   (6)
    first four pages they have completely gone out of my head and *I do not
    think of them again* until I have finished the text and then *I recap*   (3)
    wherever I need to.   (5)

F   Objectives are *relatively meaningless at first reading;*   (1)
    occasional re-reading may convince you that you have learned something.   (2)

G   If objectives are extensive and in a completely new language *one can
    experience a feeling of 'good heavens — another lot!'* particularly if the   (4)
    course to date has been a bit of a slog! They would mean more *if
    integrated at strategic points* in the text, *and reproduced at the end*   (2)
    of the text. The Study Chart is an excellent introduction to the text   (5)
    and helpful, more so than the list of objectives.

H   *Extremely useful for guidance* and if, *after reading the text, you can go* (6)
    back to the list of objectives and honestly say you understand them,   (5)
    I feel you have gleaned the required information from the text.

I   Normally I find objectives *useful, because they give some indication*   (6)
    of the nature of the text and what it is all about. My reaction on reading
    these objectives is one of *horror*   (4)
    as it is a *completely new language to me.*   (1)

J   I find that all the objectives together *create confusion* so I tend not to   (1, 4)
    take them very seriously. If they were *added into the text,* then I feel   (2)
    that I would get more benefit from them.

K   *I found that I have covered a number of the true and false statements
    in the first objective before and I have made notes on those I need more
    information about. The objectives from nine onwards will be new ground.*   (6)

Figure 6.3 *(contd.)*

L   If you understand the contents of the text (in my case this means if they
    are non-technical) the list of objectives is useful. *If contents are (in my
    case) technical, they don't signify very much* i.e. 'combining power'   (1)
    means no more than 'valency' because I don't understand either,
    therefore objectives would be more useful to me if they were *integrated
    into the text at points where they make sense.* For objectives in general —   (2)
    very useful to show the way if you understand their meaning.   (6)

M   *I tend to treat objectives only as a preamble to the main text* and feel   (3)
    that they will be *more beneficial to me at a later stage of my study
    (e.g. revision time).*   (5)

N   *I refer to them during reading of the text* to tell which aspects are   (2)
    important. *They are also a useful aid to revision.*   (5)

O   *I do not know what to make of the objectives for this text at this*   (1)
    early stage.

Figure 6.4: Content Analysis of Free Comments in FBQ 1

Comment category		Number of students
1	Objectives incomprehensible	8
2	Objectives more useful inserted at relevant points throughout the text	8
3	Objectives presented at beginning of text never referred to again	4
4	Negative affective reaction	4
5	Objectives more useful presented as checklist at end of text	6
6	Objectives useful as advance organiser	6

beginning of the text and replace it by an introduction, using
non-technical language, to give students a general indication of what
the text is about and what they will be expected to achieve as a
result of studying it.

Case Study 2: A TV Discussion

The FBQ in Figure 5.12 (p. 113) was written to evaluate a 20-minute
television programme on 'Moral responsibility'. The programme was
presented as a discussion between three philosophers on the cause of
criminal acts. No performance data were available to the evaluator, so
route III of the algorithm was followed. Items 8a-8d were concerned
with various aspects of clarity, and items 8e-8f with students' attitudes

to the programme.

The producer's purpose in designing the programme was to show how philosophy can illuminate discussion of important issues in everyday life, and FBQ 8a was intended to discover whether this purpose had been clear to the students. The responses of the 16 of the 17 try-out students who answered this question are given in Figure 6.5. At least seven of these (C, F, H, L, M, O and P) demonstrated their appreciation of this purpose.

In examining the responses to item 8b, the evaluator paid particular attention to the responses of these seven students who had correctly deduced the purpose of the programme in item 8a. Four considered that the programme had been successful in achieving its purpose, one that it had been partially successful, and two that it had not been at all successful.

In response to FBQ 8c, all students said that they had been able to follow the arguments about the cause of crime presented in 'Sergeant Krupke's song' from *West Side Story* which was used to introduce the programme, and 12 of the 17 that they had been able to follow the arguments in the three-way discussion which followed. The five students who said in 8c that they had not been able to follow the arguments responded to FBQ 8d as shown in Figure 6.6. Two points were apparent from these responses. First, students who had had difficulties found that the discussion included many disconnected examples (A, C and E). Secondly, they felt the need for some kind of summary of the arguments (A, B, C, D and E), though the expectations of A and E for 'concrete conclusions' and 'solutions' were obviously inappropriate in a philosophy course. Although this feedback represented the view of a minority of just under one-third of the try-out students, the minority was sufficiently large to be taken into account when proposing revisions.

FBQ 8e was an attitude item seeking try-out students' reactions to the programme's discussion format. All 17 students answered this item, and it was apparent from a content analysis of their responses that no dislike was being expressed of discussions *per se*, though there were many criticisms of this discussion. Taken with the response to item 8d, it seemed that most students would have preferred a tighter, more clearly structured discussion, with fewer examples being introduced and perhaps with each speaker taking a particular standpoint. In the words of one student: 'There was no real conflict, the argument did not reach a high point, and there was no resolution.'

On the final attitude item (8f), six students reacted fairly favourably

Figure 6.5: Responses to FBQ 8a

A   To show that the disciplines of philosophy are a help in understanding the premiss underlying each view — and logically weighing one against the other.

B   To show students a coherent philosophical discussion.

C   To show how philosophical argument can be used in a discussion of social issues.

D   To show applied philosophy.

E   I think the purpose of the programme was an attempt to show or teach us how philosophical debate should be shaped. Weighing each argument against another, etc.

F   To show that philosophy is being put into practice every day in ordinary arguments (but that it does not come out with hard and fast answers).

G   To introduce the idea of philosophical discussion.

H   To introduce philosophy, and show that philosophical questions are in every facet of life.

I   An introduction to thinking in different directions.

J   To show us what philosophers look like!

K   To show how philosophers do their thing.

L   To show what a philosophical discussion was like — how it is relevant to everyday issues.

M   To illustrate a typical philosophy discussion. To give students a concrete example of philosophy and how it should relate to social problems.

N   To present a discussion of the sort a philosopher might take up.

O   To show how philosophy is related to everyday life and can be applied to many of our current problems particularly crime and punishment.

P   An attempt to show us modern philosophers tackling a current problem.

Figure 6.6: Relevant Responses to FBQ 8d

A   I could not follow it all the time. Sometimes didn't see how examples followed. I like concrete conclusions.

B   It was quite good — though I found it not very concise and definite enough. The speakers obviously agreed and couldn't easily give opposite or contradictory opinions.

C   Think too many examples were covered. They should have followed through on say two of them in more detail.

D   I could not follow it because many points were not followed through as much as they could have been.

E   No, there were some instances where speakers asked a rhetorical question to open discussion and did not provide any solutions — too bitty.

towards the programme as a whole and seven unfavourably; the remaining four gave no response. Those who reacted favourably either commented on the use of the song (which they thought was an effective way into the programme) or in terms of how interesting it was to see philosophers on television. Of those who were critical, four said it was confusing because so many examples were 'thrown about' without any clear context, and three thought the discussion was too open-ended. These comments reinforced the points emerging from analysis of the responses to items 8d and 8e.

On the basis of this analysis of the feedback, the evaluator made the following suggestions to the author.

(a) The choice of topic (crime) to illustrate how philosophy can illuminate discussion of important issues in everyday life seems to have been a good one.

(b) The use of the song to introduce the programme worked extremely well.

(c) The discussion format is in principle a good way of presenting this material, but student responses suggest that its effectiveness could be improved in a number of ways:

(i) Reduce the number of disputants to two, each adopting a particular point of view;

(ii) Limit the number of examples introduced on each side in the argument;

(iii) Add a chairman who would introduce the programme by making its purpose clear to students — the chairman's role should be to both progress and halt the discussion at key points, drawing out the main lines of the argument and clarifying the approaches taken by the two speakers.

Case Study 3: A Radiovision Sequence

This case study is based on the analysis of responses to an FBQ written to evaluate a 20-minute radiovision sequence on the interpretation of aerial photographs (Figure 5.15, p. 117-18), forming part of a multimedia course in earth science. Item 11f of the FBQ provided performance data, which are summarised in Figure 6.7. On features (i), (ii) and (iv) the great majority of the students were successful; only on feature (iii) did less than the 90 per cent the author was hoping for meet the criterion. Route II of the algorithm was therefore followed in order to try to determine why this failure had occurred and to search for any process problems.

Figure 6.7: Summary of Performance Data from FBQ 11f

	Number of students answering correctly	Number of students answering incorrectly or not answering	Percentage of students answering correctly
Feature (i)	43	1	98
Feature (ii)	41	3	93
Feature (iii)	30	14	68
Feature (iv)	40	4	90

FBQs 11a and 11b were designed to evaluate students' use of preparatory materials they were instructed to study before working through the radiovision sequence. All the students but one said they had studied these preparatory materials before the programme (11a — action) and the great majority considered them to have been useful (11b — attitude). It seemed unlikely, therefore, that the performance problem was associated with lack of preparation.

Item 11c investigated try-out students' ability to see stereovision and to locate the topographical features on the aerial photographs described in the programme. The responses are shown in Figure 6.8, and indicate that the great majority of students were able both to see stereovision and to locate the features discussed. Free comments at the end of the FBQ suggested that those students who were able to locate 'most of them', rather than having been unsuccessful with some, were just unsure: this was to be expected since there was no way for them to be certain. The student who said he could locate 'a few of them only' was the same one who said he could 'never' see stereovision and who had identified all four features incorrectly in item 11f. At the end of the FBQ he mentioned that he was blind in one eye.

FBQ 11d asked students whether they had had difficulty in maintaining the high level of concentration required to work successfully through a radiovision sequence of this type and, if so, to explain the nature of their difficulty. Ten of the 44 try-out students said they had had difficulty in concentrating throughout the broadcast. Eight of these attributed their difficulty to eyestrain including, in two cases, the development of a headache. The other two said that they had become physically tired as a result of the intense concentration involved.

Some further illumination of this problem was provided by the

Figure 6.8: Summary of Data from FBQ 11c

Ability to see stereovision	
yes, always	25
most of the time	18
some of the time only	1
no, never	1
don't know	0
Ability to locate all features mentioned	
yes, all of them	18
most of them	26
a few of them only	1
none of them	0
don't know	0

responses to FBQ 11e, which was concerned with the pacing of the programme, i.e. the time students were given to use the stereoscope to locate each feature discussed on the aerial photographs. The majority of try-out students seemed content with the amount of time allowed, but 16 of the 44 found the time given to locate each feature 'too little'. This led the evaluator to wonder if the 16 students who found the pace of the programme too fast were also those who wrongly identified feature (iii). Comparing the responses to FBQ 11e with those to FBQ 11f revealed that 12 students were common to both groups. In addition, 9 of the 10 students who had had problems with concentration (item 11d) were amongst these 12.

The final item in the FBQ (11g) sought student reaction to the appropriateness of radiovision as a medium for teaching this material. Of the 38 students who answered this attitudinal item, 31 reacted positively. For example:

> On the whole, I found the radiovision programme very interesting (as it *makes* me listen!). Much better than a 'straight talk' programme.

> I think this is an excellent way of teaching.

> This programme is, I think, significant in highlighting the amount of detail that can be gained from such aerial photographs viewed stereoscopically.

Radio and stereoscope appear to be an ideal solution.

I find the radiovision aspect of the programme invaluable and interesting and feel that all radio programmes on this course should use the technique.

A small group of seven students commented unfavourably on the programme. For example:

The programme contributed little further to the course.

Did not help my deeper understanding of the subject matter.

It was interesting that five of these seven students had been achieving consistently high marks in the course. It was therefore possible that these negative comments suggested that the level of the radiovision sequence had not stretched some of the more able students.

The evaluator summarised the above data in his report to the author as follows.

It is clear from the data in FBQs 11a and 11b that most students completed the preparatory reading and exercises before listening to the radio programme and that they found this preparation useful.

All students but one (who was blind in one eye) said they could locate all, or most of the features discussed in the programme. However, FBQ 11f revealed that on one of the five photographs only 68 per cent of students identified one feature correctly, though the other three features were identified correctly by 90 per cent or more. This difficulty was not related to any inability to see stereovision (FBQ 11c), but does seem likely to have been related to problems with the pacing of the programme. Over a third of the try-out students said there was insufficient time to locate the features during the programme, and three-quarters of these were among those who made the mistake in FBQ 11f. This indication that the programme moved too quickly was supported by the fact that over one-fifth of students said they had difficulty in maintaining concentration throughout the programme.

Despite these problems, however, the great majority of students responded very positively to the use of radiovision (FBQ 11g).

Suggestion: Since the programme cannot be lengthened beyond 20 minutes, the only way of slowing down its pace would seem to be to reduce the number of pairs of stereophotographs discussed.

Limiting discussion to four, rather than five pairs of photographs would allow the introduction of more and longer pauses. This should be sufficient to give virtually all students time to identify all the features discussed without placing too great a strain on their powers of concentration; it should also reduce the likelihood of their making errors.

Case Study 4: A Student Activity

This case study is an example of route I through the algorithm, where performance is satisfactory but FBQs reveal a process problem. The activity, drawing a scale plan of a house, on which students were asked to spend about two hours, was included in a technology text concerned with 'The home'. It immediately followed another activity in which students had been instructed to draw a sketch plan of their house. FBQ 12.1 was written to evaluate the second activity and FBQ 12.2 to seek reaction to the model answer provided by the author (Figures 5.16 and 5.17, p. 120).

In item 12.1a students were asked to submit their scale plans, and these indicated that an excellent level of performance had been achieved by all students: a typical example is shown in Figure 6.9. The plans varied, of course, according to the characteristics of students' homes (e.g. a single-roomed flat, a semi-detached house, a terraced house, a sixteenth-century cottage, a large country mansion).

In response to the clarity item 12.1c, all students said the author's directions had been clear, so there were no responses to 12.1d. Examination of how students used the author's model answer (12.2a — action) revealed two different approaches. About half the students said they had used the model answer as a basis for judging how good their own attempts were: this was what the author had intended. The other half said they had studied the author's plan before attempting their own in order to see more clearly what was required.

General reaction to the activity, as revealed by the responses to the attitude item 12.2b, was mixed. The comments of several students were positive (e.g. 'stimulating activity', 'worthwhile experience'), but others were definitely negative (e.g. 'time-consuming', 'a laborious task'). The data from FBQ 12.1b helped to explain this mixed reaction. The variation in the time students spent on the activity was enormous, bearing little relation to the author's recommendation of two hours: the range was from 30 minutes for the single-roomed flat to nearly 8 hours for the old cottage (the student who lived in the country mansion spent 6½ hours on the ground floor and then gave up). Three

Figure 6.9: Example of a Try-out Student's Scale Plan

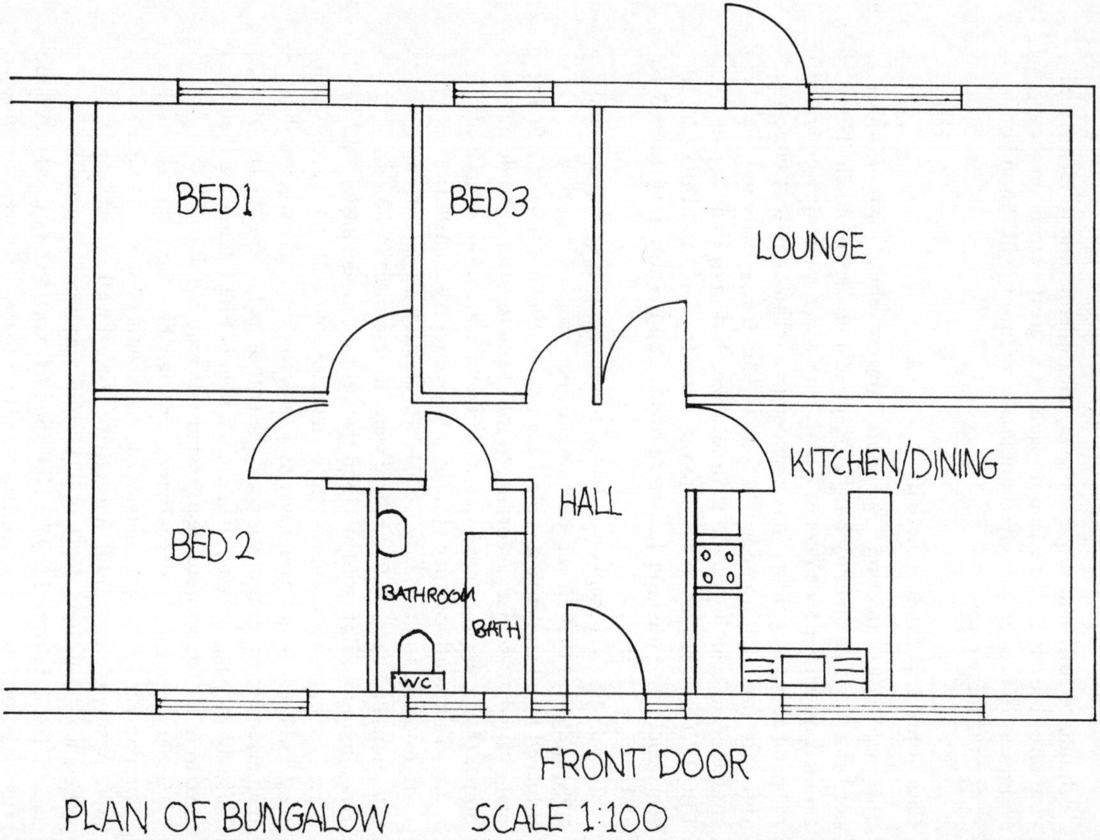

PLAN OF BUNGALOW   SCALE 1:100

FRONT DOOR

LOUNGE

KITCHEN/DINING

HALL

BED 3

BED 1

BED 2

BATHROOM

BATH

WC

students who had spent much longer than the recommended two hours made free comments at the end of one or other FBQ to the effect that the activity would have been more enjoyable if they had had to draw a scale plan of a couple of rooms rather than of their whole house: these were all students who had reacted negatively to item 12.2b.

The evaluator therefore reported to the author as follows:

Students made an excellent job of this activity but about one-third spent very much longer on it than you had intended, and some of these reacted very unfavourably as a result.

Suggestions: (a) Limit the activity to making a scale plan of one or two rooms, rather than the whole house, thus limiting the burden on those students who happen to live in larger houses.

(b) In your directions for the activity, suggest that students can use your model answer both before they attempt the activity (as a guide on how to proceed) and after they have completed it (as a check on how successful they have been).

The author's reaction to this suggestion was not what the evaluator had expected. He agreed that something had to be done about the time problem, but said that the suggested revision would defeat one of the most important objectives of the activity — to help students to perceive the *relationship* between rooms in a house, including circulation spaces. He was not very concerned that this activity should develop students' skill in making scale drawings, since this could be taught in another context. Instead of revising the activity, therefore, the author deleted it altogether, having decided that the previous activity (drawing a rough sketch plan), with which students had also been successful and which had not created time problems, was sufficient to achieve his objectives.

Case Study 5: A Literature Text

The FBQ in Figure 5.20 (p. 125) was designed to evaluate a section of a literature course on Charlotte Bronte's *Jane Eyre* in which the author tried to engage students in various activities as they worked through the text. The primary aim of the FBQ was to investigate whether students did, in fact, carry out the activities suggested by the author. Twenty-eight students provided data on this FBQ.

After studying the novel in conjunction with the self-instructional text, students were asked to write a short essay on 'The theme of education in *Jane Eyre*'. The author of the text was in general very satisfied with try-out students' performance on this assessment item.

Having performance data on the section of text being evaluated which indicated that the author's criterion had been attained, the evaluator followed route I through the algorithm.

In response to the clarity item 15d, no student indicated that there had been any problem with section 2.1 of the text, and only three students had had any problem with section 2.2. In FBQ 15e all of these three students said they had been unsure what the author had meant by 'distance' in the following passage: 'Charlotte Bronte has not "distanced herself" from her subject enough to be able to see all aspects of it with critical objectivity.'

The data from the action item 15a indicated that all but three try-out students had listed the places in the novel concerned with education and item 15b showed that, on average, they had spent 20 minutes doing this. The author had previously told the evaluator that she considered 15 to 20 minutes a reasonable time for students to spend on this activity, so this time was acceptable. The three students who had not attempted the activity responded to item 15c: one said he had not realised he was supposed to do anything and the other two had found the author's wording ambiguous, for example: 'When you say list the places in the novel, do you mean the chapters or points in the novel or do you mean the geographical places referred to?'

On pp. 40-3 of the text, the author asked the students to consider five questions which involved looking up certain episodes in the novel. In FBQ 15f, four students responded in terms of the first cue, saying that they did look up the episodes and then answered the questions in writing. Eight students responded in terms of the second cue, indicating that they had thought about the questions, but had not looked up the episodes. The remaining four students who answered this item made comments to the effect that they jotted down notes in answer to the questions without referring to the novel. The evaluator realised that part of the reason why so few students searched through the novel in order to answer the questions (4 out of 16) might have been that, having already read the novel one or more times, some might not have needed to do so. However, two students made free comments suggesting that a time factor had also been involved, for example:

I think questions like 'Can you find examples of Jane teaching herself?' should be more specific. For the time available, we need some page references. I'm not really lazy but there's a hell of a lot to get through and I wouldn't know where to start in spite of reading the book twice recently.

The responses to the action item 15g indicated that only one student did not produce a detailed plan for the essay. This student said in 15i that he had been pressed for time. Item 15h showed that students had spent about 30 minutes on average working on the plan (range 15 minutes to 50 minutes): this again conformed to the author's estimate for the activity. The attitude item 15j indicated that almost all the try-out students had found this a very useful and worthwhile exercise (e.g. 'superb', 'this sort of exercise is just what is needed', 'most instructive and necessary').

FBQs 15k and 15l were included at the author's request because, in a text concerned with literary criticism, she wanted to find out whether any aspects of her interpretation of the novel were seriously at variance with the students' interpretations. Twenty-five of the 28 try-out students responded 'no' to item 15k, and the three students who responded 'yes' made the following comments on item 15l:

> Bullying children in the name of God is not 'an evil of our time' (p. 00). It may well be in some schools in some religions.

> Reading Jane Eyre does not give me the impression that Charlotte Bronte was largely complacent about how girls were taught (p. 00). How about her criticism of Miss Scatcherd and others like her: 'Eyes like Miss Scatcherd's can only see these minute defects and are blind to the brightness of the orb'?

> We should not deduce that C.B. was not interested in current theories of teaching because she does not 'bother' to tell us how Adele was taught (p. 00). The climax of the story has been reached and artistically she had no reason to string the novel out longer. She is tying up loose ends.

Content analysis of the free comments made by try-out students at the end of the FBQ showed a great majority of very positive feelings. Only two were negative. The student who was pressed for time and did not prepare an essay plan thought that these sections of the text included too much material and too many references back to the novel. Another student said that though she had read and re-read the sections, she did not feel that she had absorbed *all* of it.

The evaluator was thus able to report very positively to the author about the effectiveness of these sections of the text. The report concluded, however, with the following relatively minor suggestions.

(a) A few students are not clear about your use of the word 'distance'. A sentence or two of explanation should be added on this at the point where the concept is first introduced.

(b) In the first exercise ('List the places in the novel. . .'), change the word 'places' to 'points' to avoid the ambiguity.

(c) In order to encourage more students to make a thorough attempt at the exercise which involves searching through the novel for evidence to answer your five questions, give page references to the sections of the novel where the principal evidence is to be found.

(d) The three comments of students who disagreed with aspects of your interpretation of the novel are given above. It must obviously be up to you to decide whether it is desirable to take any account of these in making revisions.

Case Study 6: A Self-assessment Post-test

The FBQ in Figure 5.23 (p. 128) was designed to evaluate a retrospective organiser — a self-assessment post-test included at the end of a self-instructional text on materials science. The author's purpose in including the post-test was to enable students to test their understanding of the main points covered in the text. It consisted of ten items varying in format from open-ended questions requiring short answers to multiple-choice items to mathematical calculations.

Figure 6.10 summarises the performance data resulting from items 18h and 18b. The third column of this table, reflecting the data from item 18h, shows the number of try-out students out of the 28 in the sample who said that their answers to post-test items were the same as the author's. Even on the test items where a relatively large proportion of students had been successful (items 1, 6, 7 and 8), the percentage ranged only from 54 to 64. On the open-ended questions, some students noted that they had written partially correct answers. For example, item 4 and the author's answer are shown in Figure 6.11. Only one student answered completely correctly; the other six students who attempted this item correctly identified only the first two of the author's points. Three of these commented that if the author had wanted them to note four points he should have said so. Performance was clearly unacceptable and route II through the algorithm was followed.

The fourth column of the table in Figure 6.10 indicates that this poor performance reflected, in part, the considerable number of students who had not attempted some or all of the post-test items. The

Figure 6.10: Summary of Data from FBQs 18h and 18b

Post-test item	Type of item	Number of students (out of 28) whose answer was same as author's	Number of students (out of 28) who attempted item
1	calculation	16	17
2	calculation	11	15
3	calculation	11	16
4	open-ended	1	8
5	multiple choice	12	14
6	multiple choice	18	18
7	calculation	17	20
8	calculation	15	19
9	open-ended	5	8
10	open-ended	7	7

Figure 6.11: Post-test Item 4

Question

Thinking in terms of stress concentration, cracks and dislocation, how in principle do you think solids could be made stronger? Do not consider the structural mechanisms required.

Author's Specimen Answer

1. The most obvious thing to do is to ensure that the solid does not contain cracks, either internally or on the surface; this is why whiskers are so strong.
2. The surfaces of solids should also be perfectly smooth, that is, they should contain no surface steps which act as concentrations of stress.
3. If cracks and surface steps cannot be prevented (and in practice they cannot for bulk solids) the radius of curvature at their tips should be increased so that they become less potent stress concentrations.
4. In ductile metals, the higher the stress required to move dislocations then the stronger is the material. So, dislocation movement must be made difficult.

data from FBQs 18a-18c, taken together with a number of responses to the 'Any other comments?' section of the FBQ, suggested that the try-out students could be divided into three groups. The first group consisted of about one-quarter of the students who wrote their answers to *all* of the post-test items. These students said that they had tried to answer all of the items because they had been impressed by the author's stress on the importance of doing so. The second group, also consisting of about one-quarter of the students, did not answer *any* of the test items. These students said that they accorded low priority to answering self-assessment questions: they preferred to spend their time working on the assignment that would count towards their grades for the course. The third group, the remaining half of the students, had answered *some* of the post-test items. As can be seen from Figure 6.10, they tended to answer the multiple-choice items and those involving mathematical calculations, and to leave out the open-ended items. In examining the other FBQs, therefore, the evaluator first set out to discover in more detail possible reasons for so many students declining to try some or all of the post-test items and to search for possible ways of overcoming this problem.

Over half the students responded 'no' to item 18d, indicating that some, at least, of the post-test questions had been unclear to them. Responses to item 18e indicated that the main source of concern had been the open-ended questions (4, 8 and 10). Students' comments indicated that they were not clear *what* these questions were asking, and/or *how* to answer them (for example, whether a sentence-long or page-long answer was required). Some students also made comments in response to FBQ 18e to the effect that it was not clear to them *why* it was important to answer some of the questions.

This last point also emerged in some of the responses to FBQ 18k. Whereas those students who attempted all or most of the post-test said that it had been helpful to them in assessing their understanding of the material in the text, the majority said it had not. Some of these said that they could not see a relationship between the post-test items and the list of objectives which had introduced the text. Several said they would have been more inclined to try items if they had enabled them to assess themselves on objectives which would ultimately play a part in their overall course assessment. These comments helped to illuminate the pattern of response and non-response to the post-test which the evaluator had identified from FBQs 18a-18c and began to suggest possible revision strategies.

The data from FBQs 18f and 18g indicated that answers to the multiple-choice items and the calculations had been clear to most students, but that those to the three open-ended questions had not been clear to many. Some students noted particular detailed points which were unclear, e.g. 'What does "dislocations can cross grain boundaries" mean in the answer to question 9?'

In response to FBQ 18j, several students commented that they did not know what to do when they got a wrong answer to a post-test question. This seemed to be particularly worrying to those students who had attempted all of the items in the post-test, who felt that re-reading the same material again had not helped them to diagnose their problems.

On the basis of the above data, the evaluator made the following suggestions to the author for revisions.

(a) Include a rationale for answering each post-test item which links it back to the objectives set out at the beginning of the text and relates it forward to students' end-of-course assessment (e.g. 'This item tests objective x which will be assessed by a similar type of question at the end of the course').

(b) Give students a realistic estimate of the time they should spend attempting each answer.

(c) Change the wording and format of the open-ended questions to give students a clearer idea of the type of answer expected of them (e.g. provide a space for the answer appropriate to the length of answer required; and/or give an indication of the length of answer expected in words; and/or tell students how many separate points they are expected to mention).

Thus feedback from the process FBQs investigating clarity, action and attitude enabled the evaluator to suggest revisions designed to encourage more students to make a serious attempt at all items of the post-test. What was not clear from this FBQ was what revisions the author could undertake to attempt to improve on the poor performance reflected by the data from FBQ 18h. However, a good deal of data had been accumulated from FBQs relating to the main body of this materials science text pointing to revisions to remedy weaknesses in the teaching and the data from FBQ 18i, giving students' wrong answers to post-test items, added to this information, and also enabled a further recommendation for revision to be made:

(d) Use the data from FBQ 18i on wrong answers to modify the discussions following your specimen answers to the post-test items, offering suggestions on how students can attempt to remediate their errors. For example, on item 2 all students who attempted the question correctly calculated the moments about the right-hand and left-hand ends of the plank, but four went wrong on the moments about the middle of the plank. In this case, you might say something like 'If you got the moments about the two ends of the plank correct but went wrong on the moments about the middle of the plank, your mistake may be due to. . .I suggest that you try. . .'

Try-out of this particular text had revealed very severe problems throughout, as reflected in performance on the post-test. The evaluator was able to make many suggestions for revision, but his report concluded with the suggestion that a second cycle of try-out should be undertaken if possible.

Making Sense of Revisions

The revisions arising out of the six case studies are summarised in Figure 6.12. Like the revisions in the music course examples (pp. 135-7), these fall into four categories: *adding, deleting, moving* or *modifying* some aspect or component of the learning material. Thus in Case Study 1, for example, there are instances of *moving* and *modifying* objectives, and amongst the music course revisions an example of *deleting* an objective (p. 136). Though no instance of *adding* an objective occurs in the revisions discussed in this chapter, such a revision would certainly be possible. Similarly, in Case Study 5 there are instances of *adding* and *modifying* instructions, and another instance of *modifying* instructions occurs in Case Study 4. *Deleting* and *moving* instructions are also possible revisions, though they do not occur in these case studies.

This classification of revisions can be represented on a matrix with the four categories of revision action along one dimension and various aspects and components of the learning material along the other (Figure 6.13). Global aspects of the material such as pacing and format (style and layout would be other examples) can only be *modified*. Detailed components, such as objectives, optional routes, explanations and activities, can generally be *added, deleted, moved* or *modified*. The crosses in the matrix represent all the revisions exemplified in this chapter (both in the six case-studies and in the examples from the music course on pp. 135-7).

Figure 6.12: Summary of Revisions from the Six Case Studies

Case Study 1

    (1)   *Move* the list of objectives to the end of the text

    (2)   *Add* an introduction (in place of a formal list of objectives)

    (3)   *Move* each objective to an appropriate place within the text (to the end of the section to which each relates)

    (4)   *Modify* the wording of an objective

Case Study 2

    (5)   *Modify* the format of a television programme (by reducing the number of disputants in a discussion and adding a chairman)

    (6)   *Delete* some of the examples

Case Study 3

    (7)   *Modify* the pacing of a radiovision programme (by reducing the number of tasks students are required to do)

Case Study 4

    (8)   *Delete* an activity (the scale drawing)

    (9)   *Modify* the instructions (for the activity)

Case Study 5

    (10)   *Add* more explanation (to help clarify a confusing term)

    (11)   *Modify* the instructions (for a self-assessment question)

    (12)   *Add* instructions (page references)

Case Study 6

    (13)   *Add* an introduction (a rationale for post-test items)

    (14)   *Modify* the format of open-ended post-test questions (indicating number of points required in answers and providing space for answers or estimate of length of answers)

    (15)   *Modify* specimen answers to self-assessment questions

---

Figure 6.13: A Revision Matrix

	COMPONENTS									ASPECTS	
	Objectives	Introduction	Section of teaching	Optional route	Explanation	Example	Instructions	Activity	Specimen answer	Format	Pacing
ADD		x x		x	x		x			/////	/////
DELETE	x					x		x		/////	/////
MOVE	x x		x							/////	/////
MODIFY	x				x		x x		x	x x	x

This matrix is not intended as a complete taxonomy of revisions, but rather as a formative evaluator's personal checklist of possible revisions. The search for appropriate revisions, as was emphasised at the beginning of this chapter, is essentially a creative process. Every revision situation encountered in student try-out is different, and the authors have found it useful to build up a personal 'memory store' of revisions. As each new problem is presented by student try-out, the matrix suggests the range of possible alternative revisions which can be considered. Other formative evaluators may find such a procedure useful.

7 THE EFFECTIVENESS OF STUDENT TRY-OUT

During the last 15 years or so, there have been a considerable number of attempts to investigate whether learning materials revised in the light of student try-out are more effective than their prototype versions. Many of these studies have been concerned with programmed textual materials (Silberman *et al.*, 1964; Robeck, 1965; Baker, 1970; Light and Reynolds, 1972; Robinson 1972; Kandaswamy *et al.*, 1976). A number have involved audiovisual materials of various kinds: filmstrips (VanderMeer, 1964; VanderMeer and Montgomery, 1964; VanderMeer and Thorne, 1964); tape-slide sequences (Sulzen, 1972); films (Fleming, 1963; Markle, 1965; VanderMeer *et al.*, 1965); and television (Gropper and Lumsdaine, 1961; Gropper, 1967; Rosen, 1968). Others have investigated computer-assisted learning (Rayner, 1972), simulations and games (Semmel and Thiagarajan, 1974), and various multimedia learning systems (Abedor, 1972; Henderson *et al.*, 1977; Nathenson *et al.*, 1977). The results of these studies will be summarised briefly in this chapter.

In many of these studies individual teachers or curriculum development teams have collected try-out data and used it to prepare one revised version of materials which they themselves have developed. These may be described as 'single revision' studies. They are to be distinguished from those studies which have involved the preparation of a number of alternative revisions of the same prototype using the same try-out data ('multiple revision' studies).

Single Revision Studies

The majority of single revision studies have tested revisions based solely on inferences drawn from performance data.

1. Gropper and Lumsdaine (1961) prepared two television lessons on general science topics and revised them in the light of the test performance of one class which had viewed the prototype versions. The revised and original lessons were then transmitted simultaneously on different television channels, each to 60 classes. Classes which viewed the revised versions scored on average between 6 and 26 percentage points higher on each test item than those who viewed the original versions.

2. In a later study, Gropper (1967) collected test data on another television science lesson from a try-out group and prepared two alternative revisions, one designed to facilitate retention of science concepts and principles, and the other to facilitate transfer of the concepts and principles learned to new contexts. In both cases, the performance level was raised by roughly 30 per cent over the original.

3. VanderMeer and Thorne (1964) undertook revision of a filmstrip *The Sun and its Planets* in the light of data from a multiple-choice test administered to students after they had viewed the prototype version. The original and revised filmstrips were then compared by showing them to two matched groups of students and again administering the test. The revised version did not result in statistically significantly higher numbers of correct responses to test items than the original version. Some revised frames did lead to more correct answers on the related test items, but other revisions led to no change, and a few had a detrimental effect. A further revision of the filmstrip was undertaken using the test data collected in comparing the first revision with the original (VanderMeer, 1964). This time, of four groups of students who saw the revised version, three achieved significantly higher mean test scores than those who saw the prototype.

4. Using the same try-out procedure, VanderMeer and Montgomery (1964) conducted a single revision of another filmstrip *The Earth's Satellite: The Moon*. Of three groups of students who saw the revised version, the mean post-test scores of two were significantly better than those of students who saw the original version.

5. In another study, VanderMeer *et al.* (1965) attempted to improve two films, using similar techniques to those used in improving the filmstrips, i.e. by systematically modifying them on the basis of test results. Students viewing the revised versions showed an average 8 per cent gain in test scores over those who had viewed the original versions.

6. In a rather more ambitious project than any of the above, Light and Reynolds (1972) used student try-out to improve an individualised mathematics curriculum designed for use throughout all grades in an elementary school. The methodology was again to collect test results

from the try-out group and to infer appropriate revisions. Results indicated that, in the year in which the revised materials were first used, student performance was substantially better across all grades than in the previous year when the unrevised materials had been used.

As indicated in Chapter 3, the collection of performance data alone during try-out is of limited value, primarily because it requires a high level of inference in the design of revisions. Of rather more interest than the above studies, therefore, are a number of investigations using individual try-out of the clinical, face-to-face kind described by Markle (1967) as developmental testing.

1. Silberman *et al.* (1964) described the effects of the revision of four programmed texts (in reading, arithmetic, Spanish and geometry) in terms of the comparative performance of matched groups of students studying the original and revised materials. In each case the revisions resulted from iterative individual try-out involving up to 29 tutorial sessions, and typically involved adding more frames, both in the linear sequence and in the form of branches. All four of the revised programmes led to statistically significant increases in mean post-test scores.

2. Robeck (1965) compared two revisions of a programmed text in elementary logic prepared in the light of data obtained from two successive individual try-outs. Three matched groups of students studied the prototype programme and the two revised programmes. The mean post-test performance after studying the revised versions was in both cases significantly better than that after studying the prototype ($p < .05$ and $p < .01$ respectively). The mean scores for the two revised versions, however, did not differ significantly.

3. Fleming (1963) used the individual try-out approach to improve a science film, both at the storyboard stage and at later stages of production. The effectiveness of each version was examined by means of a test linked to the film's objectives, and Fleming concluded: 'We can say with considerable confidence that we improved the film a specific 20%'.

4. A detailed account was given by Markle (1965) of the use of try-out in developing a film for teachers about programmed instruction.

Data from individual try-outs were used at the stage of developing the script, whilst group try-out data were used when developing the roughcut version into the final product. A gradual improvement in the teachers' criterion performance was achieved as the product evolved.

In addition to the studies described above, which suggest some measure of success both for try-out procedures based on deducing revisions from test results and for those based on clinical, individual try-out methods, there is one report in the literature (Abedor, 1972) of the validation of a try-out system using a more eclectic data-collection procedure. This involved pre- and post-testing of students, completion of a rating scale to measure their perceptions of lesson difficulties and strengths, and face-to-face group debriefing sessions. One developer participated in the try-out of three of his multimedia lessons (A_1, A_2 and A_3), another in one (B_1), and a third in one (C_1). After try-out of lessons A_3 and C_1 the developer considered the prototype to be adequate, and no revision was undertaken. The other three lessons were revised by their developers in the light of try-out data. A control group studied each of the prototypes of these lessons, and a matched experimental group the revised versions. On lessons A_1, A_2 and B_1 the revised versions produced significantly higher post-test scores than the prototypes ($p < .05$ or $p < .01$ in each case).

Multiple Revision Studies

The validity of the above studies as demonstrations that student try-out can bring about improvements in learning materials, in terms of increased student performance, has been questioned by Baker and Alkin (1973). Two problems arise. First, it is argued that the studies are inevitably confounded, in that the unarticulated and/or unintended bias of the single individuals or teams responsible for revising the materials might have enhanced the revised versions. Secondly, there is little evidence that the revisions made in these studies were controlled by the try-out data: the studies merely demonstrate that, after collecting some try-out data, 'someone did something' to improve the learning materials.

These criticisms are at least partially answered by a further group of studies in which several revisions were prepared by different revisers who had been given training in revision techniques and who were required to derive their revisions from the same try-out data.

1. Rosen (1968), in a study primarily concerned with comparing the effectiveness of student try-out with that of expert appraisal, had ten revisers prepare ten videotaped supplements to a preliminary version of a television lesson on English money in the light of test data obtained from try-out of the unrevised lesson. The original version and the ten revisions were tested in elementary school classes, and the mean scores of those classes viewing the revisions were significantly higher than that of the class which viewed the original version ($p < .01$).

2. Baker (1970) asked each of ten programmers involved in a graduate course to produce a programme (on any subject) for elementary school children, consisting of at least 50 frames together with pre- and post-tests. Each programmer then conducted two individual try-outs, summarised the data obtained, and prepared a report including descriptions of entry skills, frame error rates and test performance. The first draft programmes with their try-out reports were then exchanged between the ten programmers and, using a set of revision rules provided by Baker, each programmer prepared a revision. The ten prototype programmes and the ten revisions were each studied by a group of at least three children. Leaving aside the three programmes which resulted in test scores of 90 per cent or better in first draft form, the mean test score for the remaining seven first draft programmes was 3.74 (out of 10) and that for the revised programmes was 5.37, an improvement significant beyond the $p = .01$ level.

3. As part of a study of the multiple revision of six military training programmes, Sulzen (1972) found that student performance on all revised versions (prepared by trained revisers) was significantly better than on the unrevised versions ($p < .01$).

4. Robinson (1972) found that revisions of a linear programmed text on problem-solving for elementary school children prepared by trained revisers led to significantly better performance than revisions prepared by untrained revisers ($p < .001$). Although no comparisons were made with the prototype, versions prepared by trained revisers in the light of student try-out data led to significantly better performance ($p < .001$) than revisions prepared without the benefit of try-out data.

5. Kandaswamy *et al.* (1976), in a study designed to compare the effectiveness of individual try-out and group try-out, asked four revisers to prepare a total of eight different revisions of a programmed algebra lesson. Four of the revisions were based on group try-out data and four on individual try-out data. The eight revisions and the prototype were each studied by matched groups of ten students. The mean post-test score for the prototype was 8.94 (out of 33), whereas the mean scores for the various revisions ranged from 17.0 to 21.6: every revision was significantly better than the prototype (p < .001). On average, the four revisions based on individual try-out data were not significantly different from the four revisions based on group try-out data in terms of mean post-test performance. However, the revisions produced by different revisers did significantly differ in effectiveness (p < .01).

An Overview

Several questions are left unanswered by all of the studies reviewed above. First, even the 'multiple revision' studies leave some room for doubt as to how far the revision process has been guided by the actual try-out data and how far by the intuitions and insights of the reviser (q.v. Baker, 1970). At the very least, however, it seems clear that try-out data provide a valuable stimulus for such intuitions and insights. Secondly, it is rarely possible to relate a particular performance gain to a specific revision. For example, any one of a number of revisions may be responsible for a reported improvement in performance or a few rather minor revisions may have a cumulative and quite disproportionate effect on performance, a point noted by Sherwin and Isenson (1967) in the entirely different context of the development of military technology. Thirdly, none of these studies demonstrates the *generalisable* utility of try-out. Indeed, as Forman *et al.* (1976) argue, it is improbable that research can either support or disconfirm the proposition that, in principle, formative evaluation should be undertaken, since the notion of generalisability seems to be antithetical to the primary purpose of formative evaluation, which is to serve the particular needs of each project.

However, the cumulative evidence from these studies does seem to establish an overwhelming case that student try-out *can* improve the effectiveness of learning materials, as measured by student post-test performance. The question then arises as to *how* effective try-out has been in these studies. Unfortunately, the data provided in the reports do not always permit this question to be answered. Many studies report only the significance level of performance gains, implying no more than rejection of the somewhat simplistic null hypothesis that the revised version(s) will not be superior to the original version. Others quote the performance gain only in percentage terms. This, too, is inadequate, since a mean increase in post-test score from, say, 10 to 15 per cent is evidently qualitatively different from an increase from 60 to 90 per cent, though both represent a gain of 50 per cent.

A more useful measure is the 'adjusted gain score', defined by Lawson (1974) as:

$$\text{Adjusted gain score} = \frac{\overline{X}_R - \overline{X}_O}{\text{Max} - \overline{X}_O}$$

where $\overline{X}_R$ = mean post-test score on revised version,

$\overline{X}_O$ = mean post-test score on original version, and

Max = maximum post-test score.

The advantage of this index is that it measures only the additional performance which is attributable to revision of the learning materials. An adjusted gain score of zero indicates that the revision has not affected performance at all, whereas a score of unity indicates that the revision has resulted in perfect performance in terms of the criterion measured by the test. A negative score would indicate that the revision has adversely affected performance.

Adjusted gain scores are shown in Figure 7.1 for all those studies reviewed above where data are provided which make the calculation possible. The range is wide, from 0.05 for VanderMeer and Thorne's (1964) unsuccessful first revision of their filmstrip to 1.00 for one of Abedor's (1972) multimedia lessons. One point is of particular interest. With the exception of Light and Reynolds' (1972) study, the adjusted gain scores for all those basing revisions only on the analysis of performance data collected in try-out are lower (0.05 to 0.22) than for those utilising a wide range of try-out data to generate revisions (0.24 to 1.00). This lends considerable support to the point made in Chapter 3 that the type of try-out data collected should include, but not be confined to, performance data.

One of the weaknesses of the great majority of studies described above, however, is that the effectiveness of revisions is usually described only in terms of improved student performance on post-tests. Though the criterion of student performance is an important one, not all

Figure 7.1: Comparative Effectiveness of Try-out

	Adjusted gain score
Performance data only	
VanderMeer and Thorne (1964)	0.05
VanderMeer (1964)	0.13
VanderMeer and Montgomery (1964)	0.13
Gropper and Lumsdaine (1961)	0.15 − 0.16
Baker (1970)	0.26
Light and Reynolds (1972)	0.49
Performance data plus	
Abedor (1972), lesson A_2	0.24
Kandaswamy *et al.* (1976)	0.33 − 0.53
Abedor (1972), lesson B_1	1.00

educators would agree that it should be the only one taken into account.

Faw and Waller (1976) argue that in comparing different versions of the same learning materials, attention should be paid to the study time variable. Of those studies which make any reference to study time, Rosen (1968) reported increased study time, Silberman *et al.* (1964) reported that two of their four revised programmes required longer to study, VanderMeer *et al.* (1965) noted that their revised film was substantially longer for a performance gain of 8 per cent, and Gropper's (1967) revised television lesson was twice as long as the original (55 minutes as against 28 minutes) for a performance gain of 30 per cent. In such cases, it can be argued that:

> [Since] the single most important determinant of how much is learned is probably total study time. . .it is hardly surprising that manipulations which tend to extend the period of time spent in study. . .are in general accompanied by superior levels of learning. (Faw and Waller, 1976)

In other studies (VanderMeer, 1964; VanderMeer and Montgomery, 1964; VanderMeer and Thorne, 1964; Sulzen, 1972), study times for the revised versions were reported to be the same as for the original versions and the importance of the performance gains reported is therefore not open to question. The most interesting studies, however, are those in which study time was reduced concomitantly with increases in performance. This was the case for one of the lessons revised by Silberman *et al.* (1964), and for all three of Abedor's (1972) revised lessons. In one of the latter (B_1), 43 per cent of students reached criterion in 90 minutes of instructional time on the prototype, whereas 100 per cent reached criterion in 47 minutes on the revised version. Such revisions, Faw and Waller would argue, are the most powerful.

Even more important than study time, however, as an additional criterion of the effectiveness of revisions, would be measures of differences between the learning processes of students studying prototype materials and those of students studying materials revised in the light of try-out data. Of all the studies mentioned above, only two make reference to this criterion. Markle (1965) described in anecdotal terms the elimination of certain adverse subjective reactions identified during try-out of a film. Abedor (1972), using a Likert attitude scale, attempted to measure students' perceptions of lesson deficiencies and strengths. He found that all three of his revised lessons led to more positive responses on this scale (though only on one was the gain significant). As has been argued in Chapter 3, it is valuable to collect data on the process of students' learning during try-out, and it follows that it is also important, in judging the effectiveness of try-out, to attempt to discover in what way, if at all, revisions have affected this learning process. Unlike performance and study time, students' perceptions of their learning experiences are not easily quantifiable. It is nevertheless important to examine this criterion of the effectiveness of try-out in descriptive terms.

The case study which forms the remainder of this chapter examines the effectiveness of revisions made to a substantial set of multimedia learning materials using data collected by means of the integrated feedback system for student try-out outlined in Chapters 3 and 4 and elaborated in Chapters 5 and 6. All three of the criteria discussed above are examined: student performance, the extent and nature of learning difficulties experienced by students, and study time.

A Case Study[1]

Elements of Music is a half-credit second-level course developed at the Open University for first presentation in 1977, when about 1,000 students were enrolled.

The aim of this course is to familiarize students thoroughly with the elements of music, develop aural perception, teach score-reading, and give them the technical knowledge to practise harmonic and stylistic analysis of the period between about 1730 and 1900. . . Students wishing to take the course do not need to be familiar with the technical aspects of music. The course aims to provide these. In fact it should prepare students without previous expertise for third and subsequent level specialist music courses. (Open University, 1976)

'Half-credit' implies that this course should occupy students for 10 to 14 hours per fortnight over a period of about nine months, and that it will contribute one-twelfth of the six full credits which make up an Open University general bachelor's degree. 'Second-level' means that it can only be taken by students who have completed a foundation course. It has, however, as can be seen from the description above, no specific prerequisites.

The try-out system was very similar to that described in Chapter 4. Students worked through all 16 of the correspondence units in sequence, in the form of authors' second drafts which had already been revised in the light of expert commenting by members of the course team. Other components of the course (cassette tapes, a disc, set books, a recorder, a reed keyboard instrument and supplementary printed materials) were also provided for try-out students; a part-time tutor was employed to give five face-to-face sessions of about 1½ hours each during the year and to mark assignments. However, the broadcast radio and television programmes could not be made in time (Berrigan, 1977; Bates, 1978). This was a serious problem in the case of the radio programmes, since the majority of these were designed to be a central component of the course, dealing largely with aural training. The course team therefore produced home-made versions which were distributed to the try-out students on cassette tapes. The television programmes created an insuperable difficulty, and had to be omitted from the try-out programme. Fortunately, however, the course team had already decided to use television as an alternative teaching strategy: no new material was to be presented through this medium, so the absence was less critical than might otherwise have been the case.

The try-out students were selected from those who had failed to gain a place in the University to study the Arts Foundation Course in 1977, and who lived in south-west London. Since *Elements of Music* had been designed to cater for students with a wide variety of musical backgrounds, the try-out group had to include both people with no knowledge whatsoever of the subject-matter and people with some musical knowledge. Two pre-tests were therefore devised, one written and one aural, based on the skills taught in the first five units of the course. The group of 28 try-out students finally selected included eight who scored less than 10 per cent on both tests and two who scored 80 to 90 per cent on both tests, with the rest distributed fairly evenly in between. Students were motivated in the same way as normal Open University students: those who reached a satisfactory standard in their assignments and examination, as judged by a Board of Examiners constituted in the usual way, would receive a half-credit towards their Open University degree. This required a major change in academic policy within the University, an account of which is given by Henderson and Nathenson (1977a).

Feedback data from the try-out students were collected using the integrated feedback system described in Chapter 3, and the data were processed by the educational technologist on the course team, using the procedures described in Chapter 6. Reports were written on each unit, summarising problems experienced by the try-out students and indicating, where appropriate, possible alternative teaching strategies which had been suggested by them. On the basis of these reports the original authors, with the sanction of the course team, made further revisions.

The question then arose as to whether these revisions made in the light of student try-out data had resulted in an improved course. A research study[2] was therefore designed to compare the pre-try-out draft (version I) with the post-try-out draft (version II) in terms of: (i) the effectiveness of learning as measured by changed student performance; (ii) the extent and nature of learning difficulties experienced by the students; and (iii) the 'efficiency' of learning as measured by study time.

Research Design

A second sample of try-out students (Group II) was selected from the same population as had provided the earlier sample (Group I). Group II also worked through the whole of the course, presented through the same media as for Group I, some 2½ months later. They completed written feedback in the same way, submitted the same assignments and sat the same examination. The only difference was that for Group II the units had been revised on the basis of the feedback obtained from Group I.

The group studying Version I (Group I) began with 28 testers and the group studying Version II (Group II) began with 20. The dropout was exactly 50 per cent in both groups, with 14 members of Group I and 10 members of Group II remaining to sit the examination.[3] Since these students were all experiencing their first Open University course, they were comparable to first-year students taking foundation courses, for whom the dropout rate in 1976 between initial registration and the examination was 48 per cent. The reasons for dropout in the Open University are complex, but appear to be largely personal, rather than course-related.

For the purposes of the research study, it was important to establish that Groups I and II were, as far as possible, comparable. Their comparability was investigated by means of three measures, on none of which did the two groups differ significantly.

1. The previous educational experience of the students in both groups, abstracted from their application forms, is shown in Figure 7.2. Inspection of these data does not reveal any striking differences between the two groups, and statistical analysis indicates that they are not significantly different ($x^2 = 1.07$, $p > .5$ by a Kolmogorov-Smirnov two-sample test).
2. Before they began the course, all students in both groups were asked to describe their previous musical backgrounds in terms of five categories. Figure 7.3 shows the responses. Again no obvious difference between groups is apparent, nor is there a statistically significant difference ($x^2 = 1.54$, $p > .5$ by a Kolmogorov-Smirnov two-sample test).
3. All students in both groups completed the two pre-tests mentioned above, one written and one aural, before they began their studies. The results of these two tests, designed to examine students' knowledge of the material taught in the early part of the course, are shown in Figure 7.4. On both tests the mean score of Group II was slightly higher than that of Group I, but in neither case was the difference statistically significant. Nor was there a difference significant at the $p = .1$ level between the two groups's mean scores on any individual item of either test.

Learning Effectiveness: Assessment Performance

The most obvious comparison to make between the pre- and post-try-out versions of the course is in terms of the performance of the two groups of students on the eight assignments (required to be submitted at intervals during the course) and in the examination. The same tutor

Figure 7.2:[4] Previous Educational Experience of the Two Groups

	Group I n = 14	Group II n = 10
GCE O level or equivalent in 1-4 subjects	1	1
GCE O level or equivalent in 5 or more subjects	2	1
GCE A level or equivalent in 1 subject	2	0
GCE A level or equivalent in 2 or more subjects	4	3
Higher National Certificate or Diploma	1	0
Teacher's certificate or equivalent	1	2
University diploma or equivalent	3	3

Figure 7.3: Previous Musical Experience of the Two Groups

	Group I n = 14	Group II n = 10
No formal musical training	2	4
Learnt to play a musical instrument at some time	6	3
Took some form of theoretical examination in music below GCE O level standard	4	0
Took GCE O level music	1	1
Took GCE A level or a higher level examination in music	1	2

marked the assignments of both groups and the same examiners marked all the examination papers, in both cases using very detailed and highly structured mark schemes.

Open University assignments are marked on a six-point alphabetical scale which is transformed, for conflation purposes, to an arithmetical scale:

A (excellent) = 10
B (good pass) = 8

C (clear pass) = 6
D (bare pass)   = 5
F (bare fail)   = 4
R (bad fail)   = 2

The mean arithmetical grades on the eight assignments for Groups I
and II are shown in Figure 7.5, together with the adjusted gain scores.
It can be seen that version II, the post-try-out version, resulted in
higher mean scores on every assignment. With the exception of
assignment 5, the values of the adjusted gain scores were quite
substantial, comparable to and, in most cases, better than those for
the studies summarised in Figure 7.1 (p. 168). The exceptional finding
with regard to the fifth assignment, where the increase in the mean
score was insignificant and the adjusted gain score very small, is
particularly interesting. This assignment was based on units 8 and 9
of the course, the two units in which try-out revealed fewest problems:
Version II, therefore, differed little from Version I and no substantial
performance differences had been expected.

Figure 7.5 also shows the mean conflated assignment scores for
Groups I and II, the overall assignment score being calculated by adding
together the best six of the eight possible scores for each student (as is
normal Open University practice). Here again, Group II's mean score is
significantly higher than that of Group I ($p < .05$) and the adjusted
gain score is quite substantial, demonstrating the overall superiority of
Version II over Version I.

On the examination, which was marked on an eleven-point scale
(0-10), Group II again performed better than Group I, but the
difference was not statistically significant and the adjusted gain score
was rather low. In view of the much better overall performance of
Group II on the continuous assessment this may, at first glance, appear
surprising. The explanation may lie in the rather different skills required
of students in assignments and in the examination. The learning
materials of *Elements of Music* provided many opportunities to practise
the general skills required by the assignments, both by means of self-
assessment questions in the course units, and in the sense that there are
several assignments in the course. By contrast, the try-out students had
no previous experience of Open University examinations and in most
cases had only remote experience of practising examination skills in
general. Also, although the questions in the examination were parallel
to some of those set as assignments, the particular skills required were
in some cases rather different. For example, in completing a harmony

Figure 7.4: Pre-test Scores of the Two Groups

	Group I			Group II			Student t statistic
	number of students	mean score	standard deviation	number of students	mean score	standard deviation	
Written pre-test	14	33.0%	30.3	10	40.8%	37.9	0.56
Aural pre-test	14	49.4%	22.7	10	53.6%	32.6	0.37

Figure 7.5: Assignment Scores

	Group I			Group II			Student t statistic	Significance level	Adjusted gain score
	number of students	mean score	standard deviation	number of students	mean score	standard deviation			
Assignment 1	14	5.36	1.69	10	7.50	1.43	3.25	$p < .005$	0.46
Assignment 2	14	5.43	1.87	10	7.80	1.75	3.14	$p < .005$	0.52
Assignment 3	14	6.71	1.82	9	8.11	1.76	1.82	$p < .05$	0.43
Assignment 4	14	6.29	2.16	9	7.78	1.85	1.70	$p < .1$	0.40
Assignment 5	14	7.14	1.88	10	7.50	1.71	0.48	$p < .35$	0.13
Assignment 6	13	6.54	1.56	10	7.60	1.84	1.49	$p < .1$	0.31
Assignment 7	13	6.77	2.24	9	7.78	1.20	1.23	$p < .15$	0.31
Assignment 8	10	7.30	1.49	5	8.20	2.49	0.89	$p < .2$	0.33
Best 6 assignments	14	39.8	8.84	10	46.7	9.12	1.86	$p < .05$	0.34
Examination	14	5.79	2.55	10	6.30	3.13	0.44	$p < .35$	0.12

assignment, students were able to try out their harmonisations on the portable keyboard lent to them for home use whereas in a similar examination question they had to 'hear the music in their heads'. Similarly, in assignment exercises concerned with musical style and form, students could *both* consult scores *and* listen to recordings of the music, whereas in the corresponding examination questions they could not hear the music they were asked to discuss.

Furthermore, student performance in examinations is likely to be different from that in continuous assessment because of the different conditions of the test situations. Continuous assessment permits maximum flexibility: students are encouraged to plan their work well in advance of the submission cut-off date, to discuss it with fellow students and/or their tutor, and to prepare the final product in an atmosphere relatively free from tensions and pressures. Examinations are much more rigid: students are constrained by time (three hours in this case), are not permitted to discuss their answers with anyone, and, in general, are asked to work in a potentially stressful situation. For all of these reasons, it is perhaps not surprising that the difference in examination performance of Groups I and II was not of the same magnitude as the differences in their performance on continuous assessment.

Students' Learning Difficulties

Though performance in assessment is an important indicator of success in course design, so are the students' reactions to the learning process. The feedback from try-out provided a wealth of data on students' learning experiences and led to many recommendations to unit authors for changes, some major and some relatively minor. Within the scope of this case study, it is only possible to describe a few examples of such changes and their effect on students' learning as measured by the reactions of Group II. One unit, the fourth unit of *Elements of Music*, will therefore be discussed in some detail.

This is a particularly crucial unit in the course, because it begins the study of harmony, and mastery of the skills taught in it is a prerequisite for students' success in almost all of the rest of the course. The try-out data from Group I indicated rather serious learning problems, and the unit was extensively rewritten in an attempt to remedy them. Comparison of the feedback from Groups I and II indicated that considerable improvement had been achieved as evidenced by the following examples.

(a) Group I made mistakes in a large proportion of the in-text exercises (to which answers were given in the back of the unit) which were designed to practise various skills such as harmonising simple tunes at the keyboard. In rewriting the appropriate sections of the unit the exercises themselves were not changed, but the instruction leading up to them was modified, at the suggestion of some of the students in Group I, by providing worked examples with additional explanation. The effect of these changes was that many fewer mistakes were made by Group II students.

Comparison of the feedback from Groups I and II indicated other improvements arising from the changes made to these sections. On one exercise, about a quarter of Group I students made comments to the effect that they were completely lost or had found the exercise very difficult, whereas *no* students in Group II made comments of this kind. On another exercise, almost all members of Group I had taken more than ten minutes, whereas only two members of Group II had taken this long.

(b) In teaching harmony, a common problem is that there are generally several acceptable alternative answers to an exercise. In unit 4, after looking at the answers to in-text exercises, students in Group I often commented that their answers differed somewhat from those in the back of the unit, and they were uncertain as to whether this meant that they were wrong. In modifying the unit, the answers were considerably expanded to include the most common correct alternatives (as revealed by try-out) and to discuss possible variants. Consequently, Group II students expressed much less uncertainty than Group I students.

(c) The assignment on unit 4 included three exercises of a similar kind to those in the text. Both groups were asked how confident they felt in submitting this assignment. The confidence expressed by Group II students was markedly greater than that expressed by Group I students and in all three exercises Group II students scored more highly. This probably indicated the cumulative effect of the improved teaching strategy described in (a) and (b) above.

(d) Version I of unit 4 included a section summarising basic chord progressions. In response to a feedback question asking members of Group I how helpful or unhelpful they had found this section, every student commented adversely in terms of it being incomprehensible at this stage of their studies. This summary was therefore moved to unit 5, and as a result three-quarters of Group II described the summary, which was not in itself changed in any way, as helpful.

Comparison of the feedback from Groups I and II revealed numerous other instances, both in unit 4 and in almost every other unit of the course, of more positive subjective responses to Version II.

Learning Efficiency: Study Time

Open University courses are normally expected to require, on average, 10 to 14 hours of study per unit, but there has been continuing concern (Blacklock, 1976) that this norm is often exceeded, especially on half-credit courses. Consequently, members of Groups I and II were asked to keep records (in the format shown in Figure 3.8, p. 80) of their periods of study as they worked through the course. From these records each student's total study time for each unit was calculated (including text, set books, radio tapes, assignments, etc.) and hence the mean study time for Group I and for Group II on each unit. The results are displayed in Figure 7.6.

It is immediately obvious that the effect of the revisions based on try-out data was to reduce study time on the majority of units. The overall mean study time per unit fell from 12.6 to 10.8 hours. A number of other interesting points were apparent.

(a) The try-out of unit 6 revealed a mean study time of 20 hours. In fact, the extent to which this unit was overloaded was worse than this, since several Group I students reported that, in spite of long study periods, they had not been able to complete all of the work on the unit: one student gave up after 43 hours. The course team's solution was to split this unit into two (which are shown in Figure 7.6 as 6A and 6B) and to drop the originally planned unit 16 of the course. Group II still found this material difficult, but were able to complete work on it, having been allowed four weeks instead of two.

(b) It can be seen from Figure 7.6 that on five units (3, 5, 8, 9 and 12) the mean study time did not change as a result of revisions arising from try-out. On three of these (units 3, 8 and 9) no major problems were revealed and the revisions were of a very minor nature. (It will be recalled that there was also no significant change in performance on assignment 5, which was based on units 8 and 9; there was no assignment based primarily on unit 3.) It is worth noting that this provides further evidence of the comparability of Groups I and II.

On unit 5, the revisions following try-out mainly involved providing more worked examples and 'talking through' these examples at length, since it was apparent that Group I students had not mastered the required skills. The effect of these revisions was to *increase* the word-count of the unit text by 27 per cent, yet *not* to change the mean study time.

Figure 7.6: Mean Study Time

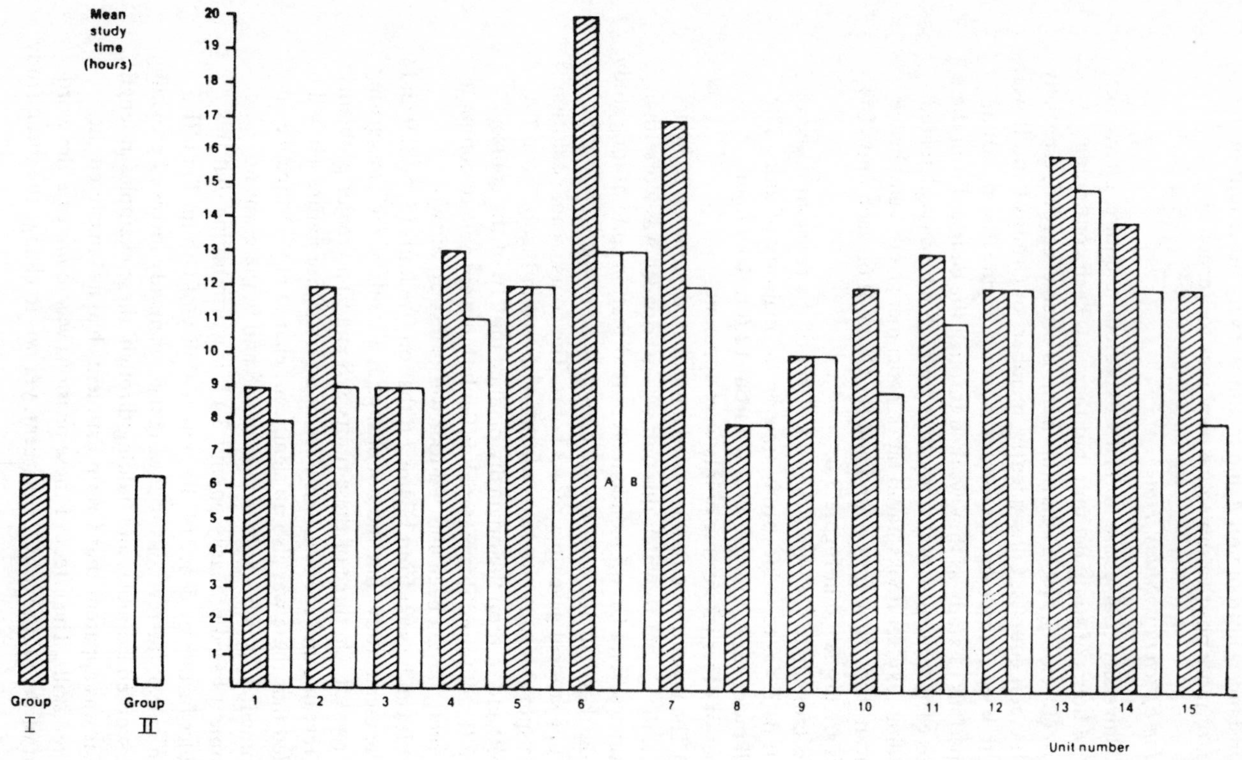

In unit 12, also, considerable revision was undertaken. Feedback from Group I indicated that some material was superfluous, and this was heavily pruned. It was also, however, found necessary to develop additional exercises to provide students with more practice in the skills being taught, and this evidently offset any saving in study time obtained by the cuts.

(c) There were several units on which the study time was quite dramatically reduced (notably 2, 4, 7, 10, 11, 14 and 15). Not all of these will be discussed in detail, but three warrant special mention. In units 2 and 4, the main changes were of a similar kind to those in unit 5 and their effect was to *increase* the length of the text in terms of word-count by 8 per cent and 26 per cent respectively, but to *reduce* the study times by three hours and two hours respectively. In unit 7 the alterations were of a different kind. Much of the material was resequenced and many of the examples and exercises were simplified: study time fell by five hours.

(d) The one unit which remained, in Version II, with a mean study time in excess of the University's norm, was unit 13. It was clear from the try-out data that Version I of this unit was too long, with a mean study time of 16 hours. The feedback gave rise to recommendations to the unit author to cut certain material and to shorten the assignment associated with this unit. However, only marginal changes were made, and the study time was reduced by only one hour.

Postscript

This case study demonstrates that the model of student try-out advocated in this book was effective in improving a particular Open University course, in terms of improving student performance, easing students' learning difficulties, and reducing study time. In conclusion, the main characteristics of the model may be summarised in terms of the ten questions posed at the beginning of Chapter 2 (p. 34):

1. Try-out followed expert appraisal;
2. Try-out was conducted on a near-complete draft of learning materials;
3. A single cycle of try-out and revision was involved;
4. The try-out group consisted of 28 students;
5. The try-out students were selected from a population resembling as closely as possible the intended population for the course, were motivated in the same way, and worked under similar learning conditions;
6. The evaluator conducting try-out worked in close co-operation with

the authors of the materials;

7. Both outcome and process data were collected;

8. Try-out data were collected both while students were studying and after they had completed studying;

9. The integrated feedback system was used to collect try-out data; and

10. The data collected in try-out were systematically processed and analysed to search for appropriate revisions.

Notes

1. The authors are grateful to the Open University and to the National Society for Performance and Instruction for permission to reprint material first published in Henderson *et al.* (1977) and Nathenson *et al.* (1977) respectively.

2. This research study was conducted by Dr Barbara Hodgson, co-author of the papers referred to above, to whom the authors are greatly indebted.

3. In the remainder of this case study all the data refer to the members of both groups who survived the course. Very similar results are obtained if the dropouts are included.

4. Ordinary level in the General Certificate of Education (GCE O Level) is a national school examination normally taken at the age of 16; the advanced level (GCE A Level) is normally taken at 18. Higher National Certificates and Diplomas are sub-degree level qualifications taken at technical colleges or polytechnics.

BIBLIOGRAPHY

Abedor, A.J. (1972), 'Second draft technology: Development and field test of a model for formative evaluation of self-instructional multi-media learning systems', *Viewpoints*, 48, 4, pp. 9-43

American Institutes for Research (1970), *Evaluative Research: Strategies and Methods* (AIR, Pittsburgh, Pennsylvania)

Baker, E.L. (1970), 'Generalizability of rules for empirical revision', *AV Commun. Rev.*, 18, 3, pp. 300-5

Baker, E.L. (1973), 'The technology of instructional development' in Travers (1973), pp. 245-85

Baker, E.L. (1974a), 'Formative evaluation of instruction' in Popham (1974), pp. 531-85

Baker, E.L. (1974b), 'The role of the evaluator in instructional development' in Borich (1974), pp. 56-73

Baker, E.L. and Alkin, M.C. (1973), 'Formative evaluation of instructional development', *AV Commun. Rev.*, 21, 4, pp. 389-418

Baker, E. and Quellmalz, E. (1972), *Research-based Techniques for Instructional Design* (National Center for Educational Research and Development, Los Angeles, California)

Baker, R.L. and Schutz, R.E. (1971a), 'An overview of instructional product development' in Baker and Schutz (1971b), pp. xv-xxiii

Baker, R.L. and Schutz, R.E. (eds) (1971b), *Instructional Product Development* (Van Nostrand Reinhold, New York)

Banathy, B.H. (1968), *Instructional Systems* (Fearon, Palo Alto, California)

Bank, A.D. (1972), *The Effect of Evaluating Instructional Products on User Test Performance, Attitude and Revision Judgment*, doctoral dissertation, University of California, Los Angeles (University Microfilms no. 72-23,772, Ann Arbor, Michigan)

Bates, T. (1978), 'Success and failure: Some earlier experiences with the pre-testing of programmes' in Bates and Gallagher (1978), pp. 7-20

Bates, T. and Gallagher, M. (eds) (1978), *Formative Evaluation of Educational Television Programmes* (seminar and conference report no. 3, Council for Educational Technology, London)

Berrigan, F. (1977), 'Developmental testing of AV materials', *J. Ednl.*

Television, 3, 2, pp. 59-63

Blacklock, S. (1976), *Workload* (Institute of Educational Technology, Open University, mimeo)

Bloom, B.S. (ed.) (1956), *Taxonomy of Educational Objectives: The Classification of Educational Goals/Handbook I: Cognitive Domain* (Longmans Green, New York)

Bloom, B.S. *et al.* (1971), *Handbook on Formative and Summative Evaluation of Student Learning* (McGraw-Hill, New York)

Bogatz, G. and Kurfman, D. (1966), *Intra-urban Unit: ETS Evaluation Report, Limited Field Trials, High School Geography Project* (Educational Testing Service, Princeton, New Jersey)

Borg, W.R. and Hood, P. (1968), *The Twenty-seven Steps in the Development Process* (Far West Laboratory for Educational Research and Development, mimeo)

Borich, G.D. (ed.) (1974), *Evaluating Educational Programs and Products* (Educational Technology Publications, Englewood Cliffs, New Jersey)

Boud, D.J. *et al.* (1975), 'P.S.I. now — A review of progress and problems', *B.J. Ednl. Technology*, 2, 6, pp. 15-34

Bray, T. (1978), personal communication

Brethower, D.M. *et al.* (1965), *Programmed Learning: A Practicum* (Ann Arbor Publishers, Ann Arbor, Michigan)

Briggs, L.J. (1970), *Handbook of Procedures for the Design of Instruction* (American Institutes for Research, Pittsburgh, Pennsylvania)

Brown, D. (1979), 'Developmentally testing the television component', *J. Ednl. Television*, 5, 1, pp. 11-13

Bruner, J.S. (1967), *Toward a Theory of Instruction* (Harvard University Press, Cambridge, Massachusetts)

Burt, G. (1978), personal communication

Clark, F. (1977a), personal communication

Clark, F. (1977b), personal communication

Clark, F. (1977c), *The Religious Perspective (Developmental Testing Draft)* (A101: Arts foundation course, Unit 19, Open University, mimeo)

Clark, F. (1978), *The Religious Perspective* (A101: An arts foundation course, Unit 19, Open University Press, Milton Keynes)

Connors, B. (1972), 'Testing innovations in course design', *B. J. Ednl. Technology*, 3, 1, pp. 48-52

Crowder, N.A. (1960), 'Automatic tutoring by intrinsic programming' in Lumsdaine and Glaser (1960), pp. 286-98

Crowder, N.A. (1963), 'On the differences between linear and intrinsic programing', *Phi Delta Kappan,* March, pp. 250-4; also in DeCecco (1964), pp. 142-52

Cunningham, D.J. (1973), 'Evaluation of replicable forms of instruction: A classification of informational needs in formative and summative evaluation', *A V Commun. Rev.*, 21, 3, pp. 351-67

DeCecco, J.P. (1964), *Educational Technology: Readings in Programmed Instruction* (Holt Rinehart and Winston, New York)

Dewey, J. (1916), *Democracy and Education* (Macmillan, New York)

Dick, W. (1968), 'A methodology for the formative evaluation of instructional materials', *J. Educ. Meas.*, 5, 2, pp. 99-102

Eisner, E.W. (1967), 'Educational objectives — Help or hindrance', *Sch. Rev.*, 75, pp. 250-60

Eisner, E.W. (1969), 'Instructional and expressive educational objectives: Their formulation and use in curriculum' in Popham *et al.* (1969), pp. 1-18

Elliott, J. (1977), *Evaluating the Educational Quality of In-service Training* (Paper presented to a conference organised by the Adivsory Committee on the Supply and Training of Teachers, Bournemouth, 17-19 January 1978, Department of Education and Science, mimeo)

Engler, D. (1976), 'Learner verification: A fine-grain analysis of go-go empiricism', *A V Commun. Rev.*, 24, 1, pp. 5-20

EPIE [Educational Products Information Exchange] (1975), *Pilot Guidelines for Improving Instructional Materials through the Process of Learner Verification and Revision* (EPIE, mimeo)

EPIE (1976), *Toward Improving National Efforts related to Instructional Product Improvement and Selection* (EPIE, mimeo)

Faw, H.W. and Waller, T.G. (1976), 'Mathemagenic behaviours and efficiency in learning from prose materials: Review, critique and recommendations', *Rev. Educ. Res.*, 46, 4, pp. 691-720

Flanagan, J.C. (1967), 'Functional education for the seventies', *Phi Delta Kappan*, 49, pp. 27-32

Flanagan, J.C. (1970), 'How instructional systems will manage learning', *Nat. Sch.*, 86, 4, pp. 65-9, 120

Flanagan, J.C. and Jung, S.M. (1970), 'An illustration: Evaluating a comprehensive educational system' in American Institutes for Research (1970), pp. 130-46

Fleming, M. (1963), 'What is a good film?', *J. Univ. Film Producers Assn.*, 15, 4, pp. 8-9, 18

Forman, D.C. *et al.* (1976), *An Examination of Formative Evaluation in Course Development* (University of Mid-America, mimeo)

Frase, L.E. *et al.* (1974), 'Product validation: Pilot test or panel review?', *Educ. Technol.*, August, pp. 32-5

Gilbert, T.F. (1960), 'On the relevance of laboratory investigation of learning to self-instructional programming' in Lumsdaine and Glaser (1960), pp. 475-85

Glaser, R. (ed.) (1965), *Teaching Machines and Programed Learning II: Data and Directions* (National Education Association, Washington)

Glennan, T.K. (1967), 'Issues in the choice of development policies' in Marschak *et al.* (1967), pp. 13-48

Green, B.A. (1971), 'Physics teaching by the Keller plan at MIT', *Amer. J. Phys.*, 39, 7, pp. 764-75

Grobman, H. (1968), *Evaluation Activities of Curriculum Projects: A Starting Point* (AERA monograph series on curriculum evaluation no. 2, Rand McNally, Chicago)

Gronlund, N.E. (1965), *Measurement and Evaluation in Teaching* (Macmillan, New York)

Gropper, G.L. (1967), 'Does "programed" television need active responding?', *A V Commun. Rev.*, 15, 1, pp. 5-22

Gropper, G.L. (1975), *Diagnosis and Revision in the Development of Instructional Materials* (Educational Technology Publications, Englewood Cliffs, New Jersey)

Gropper, G.L. and Lumsdaine, A.A. (1961), *The Use of Student Response to Improve Televised Instruction: An Overview* (American Institutes for Research, Pittsburgh, Pennsylvania)

Hamilton, D. *et al.* (eds) (1977), *Beyond the Numbers Game* (Macmillan Education, Basingstoke; McCutchan, Berkeley, California)

Haynes, L.J. *et al.* (eds) (1974), *Alternatives to the Lecture in Chemistry* (The Chemical Society, London)

HCP [Humanities Curriculum Project] (1970), *The Humanities Project: An Introduction* (Heinemann Educational, London)

Henderson, E.S. and Nathenson, M.B. (1976), 'Developmental testing: An empirical approach to course improvement', *Programmed Learning Educ. Technol.*, 13, 4, pp. 31-42

Henderson, E.S. and Nathenson, M.B. (1977a), 'Case study in the implementation of innovation: A new model for developmental testing' in Hills and Gilbert (1977), pp. 114-20

Henderson, E.S. and Nathenson, M.B. (1977b), 'Developmental testing: Collecting feedback and transforming it into revisions', *NSPI J.*, 16, 3, pp. 6-10

Henderson, E. *et al.* (1977), 'Developmental testing: The proof of the pudding', *Teaching at a Distance*, 10, pp. 77-82

Hilgard, E.R. (ed.) (1964), *Theories of Learning and Instruction*, 63rd NSSE yearbook, part 1 (NSSE, Chicago)

Hills, P.J. (1976), *The Self-teaching Process in Higher Education* (Croom Helm, London)

Hills, P. and Gilbert, J. (eds) (1977), *Aspects of Educational Technology XI: The Spread of Educational Technology* (Kogan Page, London)

Holland, J.G. and Skinner, B.F. (1961), *The Analysis of Behavior: A Program for Self-instruction* (McGraw-Hill, New York)

Horn, R.E. (1964), *Developmental Testing: Trying out Programmed Instructional Materials with Individual Students* (Center for Programmed Learning for Business, University of Michigan, Ann Arbor, Michigan); reproduced in part in Horn (1976), pp. 230-51

Horn, R.E. (1976), *How to Write Information Mapping* (Information Resources, Lexington, Massachusetts)

House, E.R. (ed.) (1973), *School Evaluation: The Politics and Process* (McCutchan, Berkeley, California)

Hovland, C.I. *et al.* (1949), *Experiments on Mass Communication* (Princeton University Press, Princeton, New Jersey)

Johnson, G.H. (1970), 'The purpose of evaluation and the role of the evaluator' in American Institutes for Research (1970), pp. 1-23

Johnson, M. (1969), 'The translation of curriculum into instruction', *J. Curriculum Studies*, 1, pp. 115-31

Johnson, S.R. and Johnson, R.B. (1970), *Developing Individualized Instructional Material* (Westinghouse Learning Press, Palo Alto, California)

Joint Committee on Programmed Instruction and Teaching Machines (1966), 'Recommendations for reporting the effectiveness of programed instruction materials', *AV Commun. Rev.*, 14, 1, pp. 117-23 and 14, 2, pp. 243-58

Journal of Programed Instruction (1966), 'Schools that have responded with educators statement as of June 23, 1966', *J. Prog. Instr.*, 5, pp. 2, 14-19

Jung, S.M. *et al.* (1971), *First Year Communication Skills Program Developed by Southwest Regional Laboratory for Educational Research and Development* (American Institutes for Research, Palo Alto, California)

Kandaswamy, S. (undated), *Evaluation of Instructional Materials: A Synthesis of Models and Methods* (Center for Innovation in Teaching the Handicapped, Indiana University, mimeo)

Kandaswamy, S. *et al.* (1976), 'Learner verification and revision: An experimental comparison of two methods', *AV Commun. Rev.*, 24, 3, pp. 316-28

Kapfer, M.B. (1971), *Behavioral Objectives in Curriculum Development* (Educational Technology Publications, Englewood Cliffs, New Jersey)

Kaye, A.R. (1973), 'The design and evaluation of science courses at the Open University', *Instructional Science*, 2, pp. 119-91

Keller, F.S. (1968), 'Good-bye, teacher. . .', *J. Appl. Behav. Analysis*, 1, 1, pp. 79-89

Keller, F.S. and Sherman, J.G. (1974), *The Keller Plan Handbook: Essays on a Personalized System of Instruction* (W.A. Benjamin, Menlo Park, California)

Kilpatrick, W.H. (1921), 'Dangers and difficulties of the project method and how to overcome them', *Teachers Coll. Rec.*, 22, 4, pp. 283-321

King, I.L. (1970), *A Formative Development of a Unit on Proof for Use in the Elementary School: Parts 1, 2 and 3* (Research and Development Center for Cognitive Learning, Wisconsin University, Madison, Wisconsin)

Klopfer, L.E. and Champagne, A.B. (1975), 'Formative evaluation of the individualized science program', *Stud. Educ. Evaluation*, 1, 2, pp. 109-22

Komoski, P.K. (1965), 'The editor's guide to this issue', *Prog. Instr.*, 5, pp.1-2, 12

Komoski, P.K. (1969), 'EPIE: Cooperative evaluation', *Educ. Screen Audiovisual Guide*, 48, 12, pp. 1.1, 24-5

Komoski, P.K. (1974a), 'An imbalance of product quantity and instructional quality: The imperative of empiricism', *AV Commun. Rev.*, 22, 4, pp. 357-86

Komoski, P.K. (1974b), 'Learner verification: Touchstone for instructional materials?', *Educ. Leadership*, February, pp. 397-9

Krathwohl, D.R. *et al.* (1964), *Taxonomy of Educational Objectives:*

The Classification of Educational Goals Handbook II: Affective Domain (Longmans Green, New York)

Krus, P.H. *et al.* (1975), 'A formative evaluation design for assessing instructional materials', *Stud. Educ. Evaluation*, 1, 2, pp. 131-7

Lange, P.C. (ed.) (1967), *Programmed Instruction*, 66th NSSE yearbook, part 2 (NSSE, Chicago)

Lawson, T.E. (1974), *Formative Instructional Product Evaluation: Instruments and Strategies* (Educational Technology Publications, Englewood Cliffs, New Jersey)

Lehmann, H. (1968), 'The systems approach to education', *Audiovisual Instr.*, 13, 2, pp. 144-8

Lewis, B.N. (1971), 'Course production at the Open University II: Activities and activity networks', *B. J. Ednl. Technology*, 2, 2, pp. 111-23

Lewis, B.N. and Pask, G. (1965), 'The theory and practice of adaptive teaching systems' in Glaser (1965), pp. 213-66

Light, J.A. and Reynolds, L.J. (1972), 'Debugging product and testing errors: Procedures for the formative evaluation of an individualized mathematics curriculum', *Viewpoints*, 48, 4, pp. 45-78

Lindvall, C.M. and Bolvin, J.O. (1967), 'Programed instruction in the schools: An application of programing principles in "Individually Prescribed Instruction" ' in Lange (1967), pp. 217-54

Lindvall, C.M. and Cox, R.C. (1970), *Evaluation as a Tool in Curriculum Development: The IPI Evaluation Program*, AERA monograph series on curriculum evaluation no. 5 (Rand McNally, Chicago)

Locatis, C. (1973), 'Some uneasy inquiries into instructional development', *Educ. Technol.*, July, pp. 46-50

Locatis, C. and Smith, F. (1972), 'Guidelines for developing instructional products', *Educ. Technol.*, April, pp. 54-7

Lumsdaine, A.A. (1964), 'Educational technology, programed learning, and instructional science' in Hilgard (1964), pp. 371-401

Lumsdaine, A.A. (1965), 'Assessing the effectiveness of instructional programs' in Glaser (1965), pp. 267-320

Lumsdaine, A.A. and Glaser, R. (eds) (1960), *Teaching Machines and Programmed Learning: A Source Book* (National Education Association, Washington)

MacDonald-Ross, M. (1971), *Developmental Testing in 1970* (Open University, mimeo)

MacDonald-Ross, M. (1973), 'Behavioural objectives — A critical review', *Instructional Science*, 2, pp. 1-51

Mace, E. (1977), *A101 Developmental Testing: Report on Religion Unit 19* (Open University, mimeo)

Mager, R.F. (1961), 'On the sequencing of instructional content', *Psychol. Rep.*, 9, pp. 405-13; also in DeCecco (1964), pp. 132-42

Mager, R.F. (1962), *Preparing Instructional Objectives* (Fearon, Belmont, California)

Mager, R.F. and Beach, K.M. (1967), *Developing Vocational Instruction* (Fearon, Palo Alto, California)

Mager, R.F. and McCann, J. (1961), *Learner-controlled Instruction* (Varian Associates, Palo Alto, California)

Markle, D.G. (1962), 'In which it is demonstrated that a program that works may well be worthless', *Prog. Instr.*, 2, 6; reprinted in *Impr. Hum. Perf. Quart.*, 1973, 3, pp. 175-9

Markle, D.G. (1965), 'Empirical film development', *NSPI J.*, 4, 6, pp. 9-11

Markle, S.M. (1964), *Good Frames and Bad: A Grammar of Frame Writing* (John Wiley, New York)

Markle, S.M. (1967), 'Empirical testing of programs' in Lange (1967), pp. 104-38

Marschak, T. *et al.* (1967), *Strategies for R & D: Studies in the Microeconomics of Development* (Springer-Verlag, New York)

Mason, J. (1976), 'Life inside the course team', *Teaching at a Distance*, 5, pp. 27-33

Merton, R.K. *et al.* (1956), *The Focused Interview* (The Free Press, Glencoe, Illinois)

Mielke, K.W. (1974), 'Decision-oriented research in school television', *Public Telecommunications Rev.*, 2, 3, pp. 31-9

Moriarty, J.E. (ed.) (1974), *Simulation and Gaming*, Proceedings of the 12th annual symposium of the National Gaming Council and the 4th annual conference of the International Simulation and Gaming Association (National Bureau of Standards, Washington)

Moser, C.A. and Kalton, G. (1971), *Survey Methods in Social Investigation* (Heinemann Educational, London)

Moss, G.D. and Chapman, P. (undated), *Evaluation of Open University Courses* (Institute of Educational Technology, Open University, mimeo)

Nathenson, M.B. (1979), 'Bridging the gap between teaching and learning at a distance', *B. J. Ednl. Technology*, 10, 2, in press

Nathenson, M. and Henderson, E. (1976), 'Developmental testing: A new beginning?', *Teaching at a Distance*, 7, pp. 28-41

Nathenson, M.B. and Henderson, E.S. (1977), 'Problems and issues in developmental testing', *NSPI J.*, 16, 1, pp. 9-10

Nathenson, M.B. *et al.* (1977), 'Developmental testing really does work', *Impr. Hum. Perf. Quart.*, 6, 4, pp. 167-77

Newey, C. (1975), 'On being a course team chairman', *Teaching at a Distance*, 4, pp. 47-51

Nimnicht, G.P. (1970), *A Revision of the Basic Program Plan of Education at Age Three* (Far West Laboratory for Educational Research and Development, Berkeley, California)

Northcott, P. (1978), 'Course teams — Some theoretical considerations, with particular reference to the Open University experience' in Northcott *et al.* (1978), pp. 15-29

Northcott, P. *et al.* (1978), *Course Teams*, Distance Education Series no. 8 (South Australian College of External Studies, Department of Further Education, South Australia)

Northwest Regional Educational Laboratory (undated), *Stages of Product Development and Installation* (The Laboratory, mimeo)

Olson, D.R. (ed.) (1974), *Media and Symbols: The Forms of Expression, Communication, and Education*, 73rd NSSE yearbook, part 1 (NSSE, Chicago)

Open University (1976), *Courses Handbook 1976* (Open University, Milton Keynes)

Open University (1978), *Courses Handbook 1978* (Open University, Milton Keynes)

Packham, D. *et al.* (eds) (1971), *Aspects of Educational Technology V* (Pitman, London)

Palmer, E.L. (1972), 'Formative research in educational television production: The experience of the Children's Television Workshop' in Schramm (1972), pp. 165-87

Palmer, E.L. (1974), 'Formative research in the production of television for children' in Olson (1974), pp. 303-29

Parlett, M. and Hamilton, D. (1972), *Evaluation as Illumination: A New Approach to the Study of Innovatory Programmes*, Occasional paper no. 9 (Centre for Research in the Educational Sciences, University of Edinburgh, Edinburgh); also in Tawney (1976), pp. 84-101; and in Hamilton *et al.* (1977), pp. 6-22

Payne, S.L. (1951), *The Art of Asking Questions* (Princeton University

Press, Princeton, New Jersey)

Perry, W. (1976), *Open University: A Personal Account by the First Vice-Chancellor* (Open University Press, Milton Keynes)

Peters, R. (1959), *Authority, Responsibility and Education* (George Allen and Unwin, London)

Popham, W.J. (1969a), 'Curriculum materials', *Rev. Educ. Res.*, 39, 3, pp. 319-38

Popham, W.J. (1969b), 'Objectives and instruction' in Popham *et al.* (1969), pp. 32-52

Popham, W.J. (1973), *Evaluating Instruction* (Prentice-Hall, Englewood Cliffs, New Jersey)

Popham, W.J. (ed.) (1974), *Evaluation in Education: Current Applications* (McCutchan, Berkeley, California)

Popham, W.J. and Baker, E.L. (1970), *Systematic Instruction* (Prentice-Hall, Englewood Cliffs, New Jersey)

Popham, W.J. and Baker, E.L. (1971), 'Rules for the development of instructional products' in Baker and Schutz (1971b), pp. 129-68

Popham, W.J. *et al.* (1969), *Instructional Objectives*, AERA monograph series on curriculum evaluation no. 3 (Rand McNally, Chicago)

Postlethwait, S.N. *et al.* (1969), *The Audio-tutorial Approach to Learning through Independent Study and Integrated Experiences* (Burgess, Minneapolis, Minnesota)

Rahmlow, H.F. (1971), 'Using student performance data for improving individualized instructional units', *AV Commun. Rev.*, 19, 2, pp. 169-83

Rayner, G.T. (1972), *An Empirical Study of a Methodology for the Revision of Systematically designed Educational Materials* (Computer Assisted Instruction Center, Florida State University, Tallahassee, Florida)

Rickards, J.P. and Denner, P.R. (1978), 'Inserted questions as aids to reading text', *Instructional Science*, 7, 3, pp. 313-46

Riley, J. (1975), 'Course teams at the Open University' in Squires (1975); reprinted in *Studies in Higher Education,* 1976, 1, 1, pp. 57-61

Robeck, M.J. (1965), *A Study of the Revision Process in Programed Instruction,* unpublished master's dissertation (University of California, Los Angeles)

Robinson, T.J. (1972), *Replicable Training in Revision Techniques*, doctoral dissertation, University of California, Los Angeles (University Microfilms no. 72-25,826, Ann Arbor, Michigan)

Rosen, M.J. (1968), *An Experimental Design for Comparing the Effects of Instructional Media Programing Procedures: Subjective vs. Objective Revision Procedures* (American Institutes for Research, Palo Alto, California)

Rothkopf, E.Z. (1963), 'Some observations on predicting instructional effectiveness by simple inspection', *J. Prog. Instr.*, 2, 2, pp. 19-20; reprinted in *Impr. Hum. Perf. Quart.*, 1973, 3, pp. 165-7

Rowntree, D. (1966), *Basically Branching: A Handbook for Programmers* (Macdonald, London)

Rowntree, D.G.F. (1971), 'The Open University — A case study in educational technology V: Course production' in Packham *et al.* (1971), pp. 64-75

Rutter, J. (1977), personal communication

Sanders, J.R. and Cunningham, D.J. (1973), 'A structure for formative evaluation in product development', *Rev. Educ. Res.*, 43, 2, pp. 217-36

Sanders, J.R. and Cunningham, D.J. (1974), 'Formative evaluation: Selecting techniques and procedures' in Borich (1974), pp. 279-311

Schools Council (1973), *Evaluation in Curriculum Development: Twelve Case Studies* (Macmillan, London)

Schramm, W. (ed.) (1972), *Quality in Instructional Television* (University Press of Hawaii, Honolulu, Hawaii)

Schutz, R.E. (1970), 'The nature of educational development', *J. Res. Develop. Educ.*, 3, 2, pp. 39-64

Scott, R.O. and Yelon, S.L. (1969), 'The student as a co-author — The first step in formative evaluation', *Educ. Technol.*, October, pp. 76-8

Scriven, M. (1967), 'The methodology of evaluation' in Tyler *et al.* (1967), pp. 39-83; also in Worthen and Sanders (1973), pp. 60-104

Scriven, M. (1971), 'Goal-free evaluation' in House (1973), pp. 319-28

Scriven, M. (1972), 'Prose and cons about goal-free evaluation', *Evaluation Comment*, 3, 4, pp. 1-4; also in Popham (1974), pp. 34-43

Sedlik, J.M. (1971), *Systems Techniques for Pretesting Mediated Instructional Materials* (Education and Training Consultants, Los Angeles, California)

Semmel, M.I. and Thiagarajan, S. (1974), 'Design, development, and validation of anticipation games' in Moriarty (1974), pp. 113-27

Shanner, W.M. (undated), *A System of Individualized Instruction Utilizing Currently Available Instructional Materials* (Westinghouse Learning Corporation, mimeo)

Sherwin, C.W. and Isenson, R.S. (1967), 'Project Hindsight: A Defense Department study of the utility of research', *Science*, 156, pp. 1571-7

Silberman, H. *et al.* (1964), *Use of Exploratory Research and Individual Tutoring Techniques for the Development of Programming Methods and Theory* (Technical memorandum 895/200/00, System Development Corporation, mimeo)

Simpson, E. (1966), 'The classification of educational objectives, psychomotor domain', *Ill. Teacher Home Economics*, 10, 4, pp. 121-6

Simpson, E. (1971), 'Educational objectives in the psychomotor ' domain' in Kapfer (1971), pp. 60-7

Skinner, B.F. (1954), 'The science of learning and the art of teaching', *Harvard Educ. Rev.*, 24, 2, pp. 86-97; also in Lumsdaine and Glaser (1960), pp. 99-113

Squires, G. (ed.) (1975), *Course Teams: Four Case Studies and a Commentary* (Nuffield Foundation, London)

Stake, R.E. (1967), 'The countenance of educational evaluation', *Teachers Coll. Rec.*, 68, 7, pp. 523-40; also in Worthen and Sanders (1973), pp. 106-25

Stenhouse, L. (1971), 'Some limitations of the use of objectives in curriculum research and planning', *Paedagogica Europaea*, 6, pp. 73-83

Stufflebeam, D.L. (1968), *Evaluation as Enlightenment for Decision-making* (Evaluation Center, Ohio State University College of Education, mimeo)

Stufflebeam, D.L. *et al.* (1971), *Educational Evaluation and Decision-making* (F.E. Peacock, Itasca, Illinois)

Sullivan, H.J. (1969), 'Objectives, evaluation, and improved learner achievement' in Popham *et al.* (1969), pp. 65-90

Sullivan, H.J. (1971), 'Developing effective objectives-based instruction', *Educ. Technol.*, July, pp. 55-7

Sulzen, R.H. (1972), *The Effects of Empirical Revision and the Presentation of Specific Objectives to Learners prior to Programmed Instruction upon the Criterion Behavior of Military Subjects*, doctoral dissertation, University of California, Los Angeles (University Microfilms no. 72-33,992, Ann Arbor, Michigan)

Tawney, D. (1973), 'Evaluation and curriculum development' in Schools Council (1973), pp. 4-15

Tawney, D. (ed.) (1976), *Curriculum Evaluation Today: Trends and*

Implications, Schools Council research studies (Macmillan Education, Basingstoke)

Thiagarajan, S. (1976a), 'Learner verification and revision: What, who, when, and how?', *Audiovisual Instr.*, January, 18-19

Thiagarajan, S. (1976b), *Programmed Instruction for Literacy Workers* (Hulton Educational Publications, Amersham)

Thiagarajan, S. and Stolovitch, H.D. (1978), *Instructional Simulation Games* (Educational Technology Publications, Englewood Cliffs, New Jersey)

Thiagarajan, S. *et al.* (1974), *Instructional Development for Training Teachers of Exceptional Children: A Sourcebook* (Council for Exceptional Children, Reston, Virginia)

Thorndike, E.L. (1906), *The Principles of Teaching, Based on Psychology* (A.G. Seiler, New York)

Thorndike, E.L. (1912), *Education, A First Book* (Macmillan, New York)

Thorndike, R.L. and Hagen, E. (1969), *Measurement and Evaluation in Psychology and Education* (John Wiley, New York)

Tiemann, P.W. (1974), 'Toward accountability: Learner verification as the next step', *NSPI J.*, 13, 10, pp. 3-7

Travers, R.M.W. (ed.) (1973), *Second Handbook of Research on Teaching* (Rand McNally, Chicago)

Tuckman, B.W. and Edwards, K.J. (1971), 'A systems model for instructional design and management', *Educ. Technol.*, September, pp. 21-6

Twelker, P.A. *et al.* (1972), *The Systematic Development of Instruction: An Overview and Basic Guide to the Literature* (ERIC Clearinghouse on Educational Media and Technology, Stanford University, Stanford, California)

Tyler, R.W. (1933), 'Formulating objectives for tests', *Educ. Res. Bull.*, 12, 8, pp. 197-206

Tyler, R.W. (1942), 'General Statement on Evaluation', *J.Educ. Res.*, 35, 7, pp.492-501.

Tyler, R.W. (1949), *Basic Principles of Curriculum and Instruction* (University of Chicago Press, Chicago)

Tyler, R.W. *et al.* (1967), *Perspectives of Curriculum Evaluation*, AERA monograph series on curriculum evaluation no. 1 (Rand McNally, Chicago)

VanderMeer, A.W. (1964), *An Investigation of the Improvement of Educational Filmstrips and a Derivation of Principles Relating to the*

Effectiveness of These Media: Phase II Revision of Filmstrip – The Sun and its Planets (Pennsylvania State University, University Park, Pennsylvania)

VanderMeer, A.W. and Montgomery, R.E. (1964), *An Investigation of the Improvement of Informational Filmstrips and the Derivation of Principles relating to the Improvement of this Media: Study no. III* (Pennsylvania State University, University Park, Pennsylvania)

VanderMeer, A.W. and Thorne, H.E. (1964), *An Investigation of the Improvement of Educational Filmstrips and a Derivation of Principles relating to the Effectiveness of these Media: Phase I Revision of Filmstrip – The Sun and Its Planets* (Pennsylvania State University, University Park, Pennsylvania)

VanderMeer, H.W. *et al.* (1965), *An Investigation of the Improvement of Educational Motion Pictures and a Derivation of Principles relating to the Effectiveness of these Media* (Pennsylvania State University, University Park, Pennsylvania)

Worthen, B.R. and Sanders, J.R. (1973), *Educational Evaluation: Theory and Practice* (Charles A. Jones, Worthington, Ohio)

INDEX